MW01483937

Transforming Darkness into Light

THE TEACHINGS OF KABBALAH SERIES

By Rabbi Yitzchak Ginsburgh
(in English)

The Hebrew Letters
Channels of Creative Consciousness

The Mystery of Marriage
How to Find True Love and Happiness in Marriage

Awakening the Spark Within
Five Dynamics of Leadership that can Change the World

Transforming Darkness into Light
Kabbalah and Psychology

Coming Soon:

Kabbalah and Medicine

Living in Divine Space
Foundations of Jewish Meditation

Transforming
Darkness
into Light

Rabbi Yitzchak Ginsburgh

Linda Pinsky Publications

a division of Gal Einai
Jerusalem

THE TEACHINGS OF KABBALAH SERIES
TRANSFORMING DARKNESS INTO LIGHT
KABBALAH AND PSYCHOLOGY

RABBI YITZCHAK GINSBURGH
Editor: Rabbi Moshe Yaakov Wisnefsky

Printed in the United States of America and Israel
First Edition

Copyright © 5762 (2002) by GAL EINAI
All rights reserved. No part of this publication may be reproduced or
transmitted in any form or by any means electronic or mechanical, including
photocopying, recording, or any information storage and retrieval system,
without written permission, except in the case of brief quotations in critical
articles and reviews.

For information:

Israel: GAL EINAI
           PO Box 1015
           Kfar Chabad 72915
           tel. (in Israel): 1-700-700-966
           tel. (from abroad): 972-3-9608008
email: books@inner.org
Web: www.inner.org

        GAL EINAI produces and publishes books, pamphlets,
        audiocassettes and videocassettes by Rabbi Yitzchak
        Ginsburgh. To receive a catalog of our products in English
        and/or Hebrew, please contact us at any of the above
        addresses, email orders@inner.org or call our orders
        department in Israel.

ISBN: 965-7146-04-0

In loving memory of our
student and friend

Rabbi Hillel Lieberman

who was ruthlessly murdered
by Arab terrorists on his way to
Joseph's Tomb in Shechem

on
the 8th of Tishrei 5761

May his soul rest in peace and
may his soul arouse the mercy
of the Almighty to redeem
Israel and all of humanity with
the coming of the Messiah
speedily in our days

"...נכון שיכתוב בצורת ספר השיעורים
שלומד. בברכה להצלחה..."

"...It would be proper to publish your classes
in book form. With blessings for success..."

*from a letter from the Lubavitcher Rebbe to the
author, Elul 5741 (September 1981)*

Table of Contents

Preface

*In the sixth hundredth year of Noah's life,
in the second month, on the seventeenth day
of the month, on that day, all the fountains
of the great deep burst forth, and the
windows of the heavens were opened.*
—Genesis 7:11*

In the *Zohar*, the classic text of Jewish mysticism, this verse from the Book of Genesis is interpreted prophetically: "in the six hundredth year of the sixth millennium, the gates of wisdom above and the fountains of wisdom below will be opened."[1] This, states the *Zohar*, will happen in preparation for the messianic era, when "the earth will be as filled with the knowledge of God as water covers the seabed."[2]

The "six hundredth year of the sixth millennium" is 1840 CE.[3] The "higher wisdom" is understood to be the inner dimension of the Torah itself and the "lower wisdom" to be the inner dimension of secular knowledge.[4]

The inner dimension of the Torah, Jewish mysticism, is generally known as *Kabbalah* (literally, "received tradition"). Classical Kabbalah describes in great detail the inner workings of reality, beginning with its own understanding of cosmology and ending with the impact of our daily actions on the spiritual worlds surrounding us.

The innermost dimension of the Torah is the knowledge of the inner workings of the soul, the profound patterns the heart traces in its ongoing search for itself and its Creator. This knowledge—which is based on the teachings of classical Kabbalah but vastly deepens it—is known as Hassidism. Although the seminal ideas of Hassidism were first taught in the 18th century by its founder, Rabbi Yisrael Ba'al Shem Tov,[5] the major compendium of Hassidic teachings that expound the depths of Kabbalistic psychology was not published until around 1840.[6]

Somewhat later in the nineteenth century, the secular world began to make serious strides in mapping the human psyche, particularly thanks to the newly-invented techniques of psychoanalysis.[7] We owe our familiarity with such terms as "the unconscious" and "the ego" to the success the insights and discoveries of this discipline have had in permeating our way of thinking.

The insights of Kabbalah and Hassidism into the workings of the human psyche are scattered throughout the thousands of works of the many schools of thought within these disciplines, couched in dozens of different contexts. In the present work, Rabbi Yitzchak Ginsburgh organizes the theories and techniques of Kabbalistic/Hassidic psychotherapy into an integrated structure, making use of the psychological terms and concepts that have become part of common parlance since the advent of modern psychotherapy.

At several points in this work, these teachings and techniques are compared and contrasted with certain well-known theories and techniques of conventional psychology.[8] However, conventional psychology is a vast field, comprising numerous, ever-changing camps, ideologies, and dogmas, many of which do not agree about even the foundations of psychological theory, let alone the practice of therapy and interpretation of empirical findings.[9] The present work is not intended to be an exhaustive comparison between Kabbalistic and conventional psychotherapy.

Some notes on conventions used in this book:

The term "Bible" comprises the Pentateuch (the Five Books of Moses: Genesis, Exodus, Leviticus, Numbers, and Deuteronomy); the Prophets (consisting of eight books: Joshua, Judges, Samuel, Kings, Isaiah, Jeremiah, Ezekiel, and the Twelve Prophets); and the Writings (the Hagiographa, consisting of eleven books: Psalms, Proverbs, Job, Ruth, the Song of Songs, Ecclesiastes, Lamentations, Esther, Daniel, Ezra-Nehemiah, and Chronicles).

The term "Torah" must be understood according to the context: in its narrowest sense, it refers to the Five Books of Moses; more generally, it refers to the entire Bible ("the written Torah"); in its broadest sense, it refers to the entirety of the written and oral traditions, all of God's teachings given to Israel to enlighten mankind.

The term "the sages" refers to the sages of the Talmudic era, whose words are recorded in the Talmud, the Midrash, and the *Zohar.*

We often use the term "Kabbalah" to refer to the whole of the inner dimension of the Torah, including the teachings of Hassidism.[10]

In the charts we use to summarize the inter-relationships between concepts or stages of a process, we place the first concept or beginning stage at the bottom and proceed upward, in order to give a graphic sense of "ascending" through the conceptual heirarchy or process.

We would like to acknowledge the invaluable editorial input of Rabbi and Mrs. Asher and Sara Esther Crispe, Mr. Uri Kaploun, Mr. Tuvya Krevit, and Ms. Uriela Obst.

May the messianic promise described in the closing chapters of this book be fulfilled in our days.

Moshe Wisnefsky
editor
Linda Pinsky Publications
Gal Einai

1
The Quest for
Psychological Well-being

MODERN APPROACHES

In today's world, people routinely turn to psychologists and psychological self-help books in search of ways to deal with their worries and anxieties. Far from being considered a sign of weakness or abnormality (as it might have been in former times), maintaining regular contact with a therapist is seen as a sign of status—it indicates that the person's life is sufficiently complex to warrant analysis by a trained professional and that he or she is concerned enough with the quality of life to be responsible about taking care of it.

This development is not a bad thing; in fact, it is not at all new. Throughout the history of civilization, all well-functioning societies have accorded mentors and consultants a pivotal role in their inherent psychological and social mechanisms for promoting stability and cultural continuity. This seems to stem from a basic human understanding that people cannot and should not attempt to tackle all of life's problems by themselves, and that there is a therapeutic efficacy in seeking help and advice from the right people.

Because the fabric of society is less tightly knit than it used to be, we are less likely to develop deep relationships today with traditional spiritual mentors. This vacuum has therefore been filled by professional therapists and other mental-health practitioners.

In recent times, along with counseling, drug therapy has become increasingly popular in the treatment of psychological disorders. Still, the consensus among psychologists is that cognitive psychotherapy is the more lasting solution for most psychological problems. Although such treatment is more involved and time-consuming (and therefore, unfortunately, often more expensive), it is generally accepted that fundamentally changing the way the patient thinks is the most effective form of treatment in the long term.

The chief problem with drug therapy is its artificial nature. Although the rationale is to provide the nervous system with the chemicals the body should naturally produce but for some reason does not, the larger question is: why is the body not producing these chemicals in the first place?

In many cases, the body may begin to malfunction because of excessive stress or depression, which may in turn be caused by destructive attitudes toward life. In other cases, the reverse is true—the body is simply denied proper care, and this takes its toll on the individual's psychological well-being. The beneficial effects of proper breathing, hygiene, exercise, sleep, relaxation, aural environment, and the like have been well-known for millennia and are also documented by modern science. And, of course, proper diet is essential to physical and psychological health.[1] In addition, doctors over the centuries have prescribed herbs to help balance psychophysical functions.[2] It is clear that many psychological problems can be alleviated or even cured simply by paying attention to these often neglected aspects of life.

Despite this, there remain many psychological problems that require more direct or intensive treatment than physical lifestyle adjustments. This is why counseling in one form or another has always been an essential aspect of most societies and remains so today.

KABBALAH AND PSYCHOTHERAPY

The system of psychotherapy we will explore here is that of the Kabbalah, the Jewish mystical tradition and inner "soul" of the Torah, as it has been expounded and developed by the great Hassidic masters: the 18th century founder of the Hassidic movement, Rabbi Yisrael Ba'al Shem Tov and his disciples and successors.[3]

In the Hassidic community, the role of the psychologist may be filled either by the leader of the Hassidic court himself (the *rebbe*), a Hassidic elder, a close friend, or some other spiritual mentor. (In many respects, one's spouse—who is ideally one's closest friend[4]—can fulfill the role of the therapist.) All members of the Hassidic community are expected to find themselves a mentor, and, with the mentor's help, work out their problems and anxieties through a program of regular counseling.[5]

In this respect, the Hassidic community may seem very similar to the world at large. There are, however, many fundamental differences between Kabbalistic psychotherapy and other approaches to counseling, just as Kabbalah and other systems possess very different visions of what psychological well-being is and how to achieve it. These differences stem, of course, from the basic points of divergence between Kabbalah and any philosophy or religion that is not rooted in the belief system of the

Torah.[6] Central to understanding these differences is how each perceives the role of self-knowledge in mental health.

SELF-KNOWLEDGE

Western secular culture has always considered self-knowledge the crown jewel of human endeavor.[7] The teachings of Kabbalah, however, give priority to the Torah's dictum: "Know before whom you stand."[8] Indeed, King David's last words to his son, King Solomon, were: "Know the God of your father; serve Him with your whole heart and a willing soul."[9]

In the Torah's scheme, the meaning of life is to know *God*, that is, to be constantly aware of His presence. Knowledge of God, not of ourselves, is meant to fill our consciousness.

Nonetheless, to know God, we must first know ourselves. Since it is impossible for the finite human mind to know the infinite God directly, we can only come to know God indirectly, by first perceiving the Godliness within ourselves. Created as we are "in the image of God,"[10] we ourselves are the mirror through which we can apprehend God, as it is written, "from my flesh do I see God."[11] Our task, therefore, is to unearth the Godliness hidden within us. Although this may not be easy, once we become attuned to the Divine dimension within ourselves, we are able to see the Divinity inherent in all creation and to sense just what our roles are in the grand scheme of things.

According to the sages, God created the world in order to have a home in "the lower realms."[12] "Lower" here does not mean physically lower, but lower on the scale of consciousness of God. In this understanding, our physical world is on the lowest rung of a vast hierarchy of "universes," or orders of existence, each defined by a different grade of awareness of God the Creator.[13] Our world is the lowest in that it does not initially betray the fact that anyone created it. Nature is so perfect a disguise for the Divine power constantly creating the world that it is possible for people to be born, live their whole lives, and die without ever discovering that there is a God.

It is this world, where His presence is so concealed, that God seeks to make His "home." Precisely here, where everything seems antithetical to our awareness of Him, He wants us to be aware of His existence and to establish a relationship with Him. This is why He created such a world in the first place, and why each individual soul is sent "down" here. Every individual has a unique role to play in achieving this goal, and the only way we can each determine our unique purpose in this scheme is by attuning ourselves to the Godliness within us. It is in this sense and to this end that we must "know ourselves."

For most of us, though, the Divine self is so hidden under layers after layers of mundane consciousness that we may well despair of ever uncovering it. How, then, do we set about knowing our inner, Divine self, so that we may come to know God? This is the goal and *raison d'être* of Kabbalistic psychotherapy, and its major point of departure from conventional psychology.

KNOWLEDGE OF GOD

Conventional psychology describes both the conscious and unconscious states of normative human psyche,[14] both of which are primarily *self*-conscious in nature. It does not focus on the knowledge of God. Although it may not categorically deny God's existence, it generally ignores God as an active determinant in mental health, and consequently, also ignores the existence of a Divine soul, an entity apart from and transcending the normative human consciousness it is concerned with.

This leaves conventional psychology in an interesting predicament. If a man is drowning in quicksand, he has to take hold of something or someone outside the quicksand to get out. Similarly, a man beset by problems and anxieties needs the help of someone or something that transcends these problems and anxieties in order to extricate himself from them. Yet the most that conventional psychology can offer the suffering soul is the helping hand of another human being,[15] or perhaps an entry into an untapped human dimension of the patient's mind. This may indeed provide temporary respite, but it cannot hope to serve as a cure, because we are all subject to the same human condition. If ultimately we are all in the same boat, who is there to throw us a line?[16]

Impressive though its successes may be, conventional psychology by its very nature cannot address or solve the fundamental riddles of human existence that underlie most psychological problems. After all, it originates in the same, limited human mind it is attempting to understand and treat. (It is this limited origin that also gives rise to its wide divergence of conflicting theories and approaches.)

In the Kabbalah, the awareness of Godliness within us is seen as the key to our personal psychological redemption from the forces that threaten to overwhelm us. God's omnipresence means that no matter how low we may think we have fallen, He is with us, throwing us a rope in order to help us work our way up and out. As it is written, "Even if I descend to the depths, behold, You are there."[17] The more we can sensitize ourselves to our Divine inner essence, the more we become aware and attuned to God's omnipresence, and the quicker we can extricate ourselves from the worries that pull us down.

Conventional psychology, not offering this unconditional escape-hatch, cannot provide the basis for people to truly and completely face the truth about themselves.[18]

2
The Process of
Spiritual Growth

SUBMISSION, SEPARATION AND SWEETENING

The existence of problems in our lives challenges us to respond to them by undergoing a process of spiritual growth.

The Ba'al Shem Tov taught that any process of spiritual growth—and, in fact, the in-depth experience of any facet of reality—must proceed through three developmental changes in attitude, which he called:

- "submission,"

- "separation," and

- "sweetening."[1]

Submission is the humbling of the ego that is the basis of any honest appraisal of reality and our relation to it. Until we neutralize the ego, it will be sure to interpose its own interests between our true self and our objective assessment of our problem.

Eliminating the deceptive self-image derived from the ego allows us to disassociate ourselves—to separate—from our problem.[2] When we separate ourselves from the problem and stop

9

defining ourselves in its terms, the good within us begins to shine; we achieve the clarity of objectivity.

We can then proceed to "sweeten" the problem by solving it. We can evaluate the bad in the positive light of the good that is intermixed with it.[3]

LIGHT AND DARKNESS

The inward process of submission, separation, and sweetening is a reflection of the interaction between light and darkness that characterizes all Divine revelation, beginning with creation itself:

> In the beginning...the earth was without form and void...and darkness was on the face of the deep.... And God said, "Let there be light," and there was light. God saw that the light was good, so God separated the light from the darkness.... And it was evening, and it was morning, one day.[4]

From this seminal passage we see (1) that darkness preceded light; (2) that even when light was created, it was still commingled with darkness and had to be separated from it; and (3) that a full phase of revelation—"one day"—is complete only when it includes both darkness (evening) and light (morning).

The creative dynamic established on the first day of creation is the paradigm for all creative processes, including the threefold process of spiritual growth taught by the Ba'al Shem

Tov. The initial darkness and confused mingling of darkness and light is the psychological problem or anxiety to which we must respond by humbling our ego. This is submission. The "light" and "darkness" are the good and bad aspects of our personalities that the problem highlights or obscures; our task is to isolate our inner light from our inner darkness and identify with it. This is separation. The new "day" is the higher way of living we create by shining the light on our problem and its root. This is sweetening the evil with the good.[5]

The duality of light and darkness in creation is also alluded to in the prophet Ezekiel's vision of the Divine chariot, the most overtly mystical passage of the Bible:

> ...the heavens opened, and I saw visions of God. And I saw, and behold, a stormy wind came out of the north, a great cloud, and a flashing fire, and a translucent glow surrounded it, and out of the midst of it, out of the midst of the fire, was something like the *chashmal.*[6]

The word *chashmal* appears in the Bible only in the context of this vision,[7] and is understood in Kabbalah to be a type of light or energy originating in the Divine oneness above time and space; thereafter, in the creative process, it becomes personified as a genre of angels. *Chashmal* is a compound of two other words: *chash,* meaning "silent," and *mal,* meaning "speaking."

At the level of Divine oneness, the level of Divine paradox, silence and speech exist and are expressed simultaneously. The silence speaks and the speech is silent. This is the paradoxical "soft, silent voice"[8] heard by the prophet Elijah. At the level of the created, spiritual world, the *chashmal*-angels are said to be "sometimes silent, sometimes speaking."[9] Here, the created dimension of time differentiates between the two antithetical states of expression—silence and speech, as it is written: "there is a *time* to be silent, and a *time* to speak."[10]

The Ba'al Shem Tov identifies a third, intermediary stage between the two extremes of silence and speech. The allusion to this stage of *chashmal* is in its second syllable, *mal*, which can also be translated as "severing." There are thus three developmental stages: silence, severing, and speech.

The Ba'al Shem Tov links these three stages with the three stages of spiritual growth described above. Being silent is an act of submission. By remaining silent, we are admitting that in our not-yet-rectified state we are unable to say anything, that we are unable to deal with the situation we are facing. We must defer instead to the authority of the Torah, which instructs us how to sever or separate ourselves from evil. Only then can we speak, that is, actively transform the evil and its root into good, thus sweetening it.

The external actions of being silent, severing, and speaking, are thus the outer manifestations of the inner, psychological processes of submission, separation, and sweetening.

mal	speech	3. sweetening
mal	severing	2. separation
chash	silence	1. submission

Speech is meaningful only when it is brought into relief and contrasted by silence. Indeed, the Ba'al Shem Tov teaches[11] that a person who is seeking a mentor in life should attempt to sense the backdrop of silence in the prospective mentor's speech, that is, to discern if the mentor has gone through the processes of submission and separation before he begins to speak. If he has gone through these processes, he will be able to sweeten the lives of those who seek his counsel and be a worthy mentor.

How does one sense this? A sensitive listener will be deeply affected by the mentor's silent contemplation of the words he is about to speak. The listener will see in the mentor's facial expressions that he is going through the first two stages of submission and separation:[12] first, the mentor feels himself empty of knowledge, not knowing what to say. If he is worthy, the spiritual vacuum caused by his humility will draw down a new flow of insight that will help him understand the listener's problem. The mentor will then proceed to separate and organize his thoughts in preparation to speak.

Then, in his stage of sweetening, the mentor will speak from his state of inner peace. In the depth of his being, he is at peace with God, having fully surrendered himself to Him. He is past the inner turmoil that results from the conflict between the ego and God. When the words of the mentor reflect this inner tranquility, they will touch the listener deeply. As King Solomon advised, "the words of the wise, spoken gently, are heeded."[13]

3
Therapeutic Techniques

Although life abounds with difficulties, healthy people cope with their problems and concerns without becoming overwhelmed by them. When a person begins to worry too much about his or her problems, whether real or imagined, anxiety sets in.

Conscious anxiety reflects our subconscious fear that we are unable to cope with what life has in store. On a deeper level, anxiety may be caused by the frustration born of the innate conflict between our mundane, physical urges and our higher, spiritual aspirations. In addition, the tension and pressure of anxiety in one sphere of life can exacerbate psychological problems in another sphere. These factors make anxiety the main reason most people seek the aid of psychotherapy.

What, then, does Kabbalah say about anxiety? The teachings of Kabbalah, as the teachings of Judaism in general, are intimately bound up with the textual nuances of the written text of the Torah. Any inquiry into the Kabbalistic approach to a particular subject must therefore begin with an analysis of what the Torah says about the subject.

Anxiety is mentioned several times in the Bible, but the most seminal instance is the following verse from the Book of Proverbs:[1]

> If there be anxiety in a man's heart, let him suppress it, and a good word will turn it into joy.

The Book of Proverbs was written by King Solomon, who, the Bible testifies, was the wisest of all men,[2] particularly in the realm of human psychology. In this verse we may thus expect to find the key to psychological well-being and the proper approach for dealing with psychological problems.

According to the sages of the Talmud, the Hebrew word for "let him suppress it" has two additional meanings: "let him ignore it" and "let him articulate it."[3] There are thus three distinct instructions regarding the proper response to anxiety: to suppress it, to ignore it, and to articulate it.

These three instructions may be seen to represent three complementary therapeutic techniques for dealing with anxiety. If they are properly implemented, we may expect these techniques to prevent anxiety from developing into something more serious, or even to cure it.

If the Ba'al Shem Tov's threefold process of submission, separation, and sweetening is necessary for spiritual growth in general, it is certainly necessary for overcoming anxiety, since attaining and maintaining mental health is a basic requirement for spiritual growth. We may therefore view the three therapeutic techniques alluded to in the verse from Proverbs as reflecting the three stages of the therapeutic process of overcoming anxiety. In this light, suppressing, ignoring, and articulating anxiety are not unrelated processes but a progression of successive techniques.

We will now examine how these three therapeutic techniques follow the Ba'al Shem Tov's general model of the process of spiritual growth:

3. sweetening	speech	articulating anxiety
2. separation	severing	ignoring anxiety
1. submission	silence	suppressing anxiety

SUPPRESSING ANXIETY

The first and most basic instruction given by King Solomon is to suppress the anxiety that troubles the heart, which means to deflate it or cut it down to size.

Suppressing the problem in this context does not mean repressing it, i.e., sweeping it under the rug by unconsciously avoiding it. Repressing an anxiety is comparable to covering a wound without treating it, which will most likely cause it to fester and re-emerge worse than before. Suppressing the anxiety, in contrast, eventually enables us to examine and resolve our problems in their proper context, as will become clear later.[4]

When we are troubled by something, we naturally tend to focus on it. We first look for a solution, but if none is forthcoming, we will exaggerate the problem's significance if we continue to focus on it. Our anxiety over the problem may eventually begin to dominate us.

J. is very worried about her health. Since she has not resolved this anxiety, it has begun to nag her incessantly. In her imagination, the fear begins to assume ominous proportions—she fears that the doctors have misdiagnosed her; that the laboratory has mixed up the results of her tests; that she has a terminal illness that all the experts have overlooked. She becomes convinced that no one can fathom the depth of her troubles.

A way must be found to put J.'s problem in its proper perspective, to silence the inner turbulence of her thought so its relevance is not overstated. The antidote to this exaggeration of anxiety is to suppress the ego. This is an act of submission, in which the egocentricity is deflected and the ego itself is suppressed.

In general, egocentricity is manifest as self-preoccupation, selfishness, or, in the extreme, narcissism. Instead of feeling indebted and grateful to God, society, and all those individuals who directly or indirectly contribute to their well-being, egocentric people think that everything they have is due them.

A psychotherapist or counselor can use the psychological strategies and techniques of submission to teach egocentric people how to neutralize their ego and free themselves from self-preoccupation in order to relate truly to others.

S. is a young, married woman with a baby. She constantly complains that her mother does not visit her enough or help her with babysitting and other household chores. She reasons that this is a mother's duty to her daughter. After all, who else is supposed to help her and stand by her side at all times, if not her mother? S.'s egocentricity makes her insensitive to the full spectrum of her mother's responsibilities to her own life and household, and she cannot empathize with her mother's physical and psychological limitations.

In this example, S.'s counselor should guide her through the process of submission. Deflating her ego will allow her to feel grateful to God and humanity, become more concerned for the welfare of others than for her own, and be happy with her lot. Instead of feeling that she is entitled to more, she will learn that she deserves no more than she has and all that she does have is solely a gift from God. The counselor should teach her to review these ideas until they become an integral part of her consciousness.

With S.'s ego out of the way, the counselor can help her realize that her mother really does love her and helps her as much as she can, but is objectively unable to respond to all of S.'s demands.

> A disciple of Rabbi Shneur Zalman of Liadi once complained to him that he had lost most of his wealth. He could no longer provide for himself; worst of all, he could no longer fulfill his many charitable obligations. The rabbi chastised him, saying, "You have described what *you* need, but you have said nothing about what *you are* needed *for!*"
>
> The disciple fainted and was removed from Rabbi Shneur Zalman's study. When he regained consciousness, he pondered Rabbi Shneur Zalman's words in depth. He forgot about his troubles and began a process of serious introspection. He began to take his Torah studies and prayers seriously, evaluate his direction in life, and feel remorseful for having ignored and betrayed his Divine soul for so long.
>
> Sometime later, Rabbi Shneur Zalman called him into his study. He told his disciple: "Now that you have integrated God's presence into your life, you can return to your home and your business. May God grant you success." And so it was.[5]

But didn't the disciple say that he needed *to give charity*? Didn't that qualify as something he was "needed for"? Evidently, Rabbi Shneur Zalman saw that his disciple's desire to do good stemmed from egocentric motives. He wanted to maintain his prestige in the eyes of his community, its opinion being a mirror of his own desired self-image.

Rabbi Shneur Zalman engraved upon the heart of his disciple that he must escape the psychological trap of egocentricity and become *truly* concerned with the welfare of others, for their sake. This is true submission.

Suppressing anxiety results in the liberating feeling that all is not lost. The problem may still be there, but it has been cut down to size and no longer threatens to crush us under its weight.

Once we have been freed from this burden, we may proceed to the next phase of therapy.

IGNORING ANXIETY

The second phase of therapy, implied by the second meaning of King Solomon's advice, is ignoring anxiety. This is much easier to do once our subjective perception of the immensity of the problem has been reduced in the first phase.

To ignore a problem means to separate ourselves from it, the second stage of the Ba'al Shem Tov's model. Anxiety over a problem can lead us to identify ourselves with it and define ourselves in terms of it.

Not only has J. exaggerated the magnitude of her health problem; she has become so obsessed with it that she thinks of herself solely in terms of her health condition. She imagines that other people refer to her as "the woman with that medical condition." Her identity as her own person—and as a wife, mother, daughter, sister, and friend—have all been subordinated to her dominant identity as a sufferer.

In this second stage of therapy, we learn to disassociate ourselves from our problems. We do not deny their existence or relevance, but we cease to identify with them.

By separating ourselves from our problems, we learn to focus on the positive aspects of life. This promotes further spiritual growth. Once we have established some measure of self-confidence in our own spiritual abilities, we are ready to proceed to the next phase of therapy.

ARTICULATING ANXIETY

The final phase of therapy, implied by the third meaning of King Solomon's advice, is articulating anxiety. This is the phase where we set out to actively solve—or "sweeten," in Ba'al Shem Tov's terminology—the problem that is causing the anxiety.

The two preceding phases, suppressing and ignoring anxiety, are prerequisite to this final phase. This is because in order to relate to something objectively and analyze it truthfully, we must first be released from our subjective ties to it.

With the help of her counselor, J. comes to understand that in order to solve her problem she must reach its root. To do this, she must articulate her feelings and analyze them in depth with another person. Using the new insight this dialogue reveals, J.'s counselor will help her approach the issue of her health in a balanced, level-headed way. Moreover, J. will learn to see herself in a new light, which will help her progress and succeed in all avenues of her life.

When we articulate our concerns and anxieties to a sensitive and understanding friend or mentor, we are well on the way to solving the problem that caused them by reaching its root. The friend or mentor can offer the "good word" that will help us "turn it into joy." The exchange of words between two people is the tool through which the conflict is resolved. As King Solomon says, "God enlightens the eyes of them both."[6]

INTER-INCLUSION

In the cosmology of Kabbalah, the present order of reality is the rectification of several immature stages of creation that preceded it. (The word "preceded" must be taken allegorically, since time as we know it began only with the present order of creation.) In the previous orders of creation, the creative forces governing them did not act in unison; each creative force pursued its own course of action without regard to the effect this would have on its sister forces or the effect its sister forces might exert on it. The result was chaos, which led to the collapse of these universes.

In contrast, in the present order, the forces God used (and uses) to create and sustain the world act in harmony; each considers the spiritual personality of all the others. This is possible because they exhibit inter-inclusion, that is, each creative force incorporates something of all the other creative forces. The presence of an element of the other within it allows it to interact with the other constructively. In this way, creation reflects its underlying "holographic" unity, demonstrating that it is the handiwork of one God.

This maturation of creation may be roughly compared to how children mature into adults. Children possess the same personality traits as adults, but these traits exist in them in an unsettled pandemonium. Children's desires and drives are powerful but immature. When children want something, it is difficult if not impossible for them to consider the impact that satisfying this desire may have on their other, presently subdued, desires. As children mature, they learn how to temper the unilateral nature of their urges in light of the full spectrum of motives. Gradually, they come to realize that they must moderate their pursuit of their own ephemeral interests in favor of larger, more altruistic and long-term goals, for the sake of which they must sort out—inter-include—their emotions. For this process to occur, egocentricity must be neutralized. The trauma this causes and the accompanying self-redefinition is, of course, a major feature of adolescence.

The hallmark of the rectified order of creation, then, is inter-inclusion. Every successful process, model, system, or organization needs to evince this quality. Conversely, any process that does not possess this quality is "unrectified": it relates to the previous, superseded order of creation, and injurious to the present order and its progress toward perfection. This, in effect, is the definition of evil according to Kabbalah.

Therefore, the potential of the Ba'al Shem Tov's threefold model of spiritual growth as a path toward rectification becomes fully evident when each stage is seen as an inter-inclusion of all three stages. Since the Kabbalistic therapeutic process is structured in accordance with this model, the same holds true for it: each of the three techniques of dealing with anxiety—suppressing anxiety, ignoring anxiety, and articulating anxiety—are present as sub-stages in each technique.

In the ensuing chapters, we will describe the full Kabbalistic therapeutic process in terms of this principle of inter-inclusion:

Submission: Suppressing Anxiety
- The Nature of Existence: Submission within Submission
- The Reality Check: Separation within Submission
- Heartfelt Prayer: Sweetening within Submission

Separation: Ignoring Anxiety
- Dismissing Negative Thoughts: Submission within Separation
- Self-redefinition: Separation within Separation
- Positive Thinking: Sweetening within Separation

Sweetening: Articulating Anxiety
- The Need for Another: Submission within Sweetening
- The Local Solution: Separation within Sweetening
- Transforming Evil into Good: Sweetening within Sweetening

The order of this threefold process and its expansion into nine sub-stages should be primarily understood as thematic rather than rigidly sequential. Although each step builds on the previous steps, each is in its own right a technique for reacting to a given psychological state. It is therefore possible to employ a strategy that pertains to a person's present psychological state without regard to its place in the sequence we will describe. In particular, any of the three "submission-within-" phases are legitimate starting points of the therapeutic process, since each is, after all, a form of submission.

In all likelihood, however, one will feel that there is still more work to do even after a particular stage has been implemented and the problem alleviated. The more sensitive the person is, the more likely he or she will feel this to be the case. This is because the therapeutic process described here is a comprehensive and cumulative one. Although a specific technique may be sufficient to solve a particular problem, full psychological well-being can result only if the full process is implemented.

Furthermore, we can suffer setbacks in our process of spiritual growth as much as we can in any other facet of life, as the Book of Proverbs declares, "the righteous will fall seven times and rise."[7] In such cases, we have to begin to climb anew from the point of regression. By working through the psychological problems relevant to the level to which we have regressed, we save ourselves from falling further and hasten our return to our former level. Ultimately, we fall or regress for the sake of reaching a new height, which we could not have reached had we only progressed, without regressing.[8]

The inability to deal with the psychological fall is surely the major educational problem of our time; most educational systems have no method for dealing with young people living through a period of fluctuating maturity. As a result, when young people experience the disorientation that accompanies this phenomenon, they develop anxieties over it, which is why classic psychoanalysis asserts the necessity to trace the source of anxiety into childhood and adolescence.

In contrast, the assertion that it is possible to serve God in a temporary state of discontinuous psychological regression was one of the major religious innovations of the Ba'al Shem Tov.

The following anecdote from his life illustrates how the Ba'al Shem Tov applied this principle even to himself:

On one of his aborted trips to the Holy Land, the Ba'al Shem Tov suddenly forgot all his knowledge of the Torah. However, he was certain that if his scribe, Rabbi Tzvi, who was accompanying him, recited some verse from the Torah or

some saying of the sages, this would serve as a kernel around
which he could reconstruct his knowledge. But alas, Rabbi
Tzvi had also forgotten everything! So the Ba'al Shem Tov
asked him to recite the Hebrew alphabet, but all Rabbi Tzvi
could remember was the first letter, *alef.* The Ba'al Shem Tov
had him say *alef* over and over; this eventually reminded
them of the second letter, *beit,* and so on, until they
remembered the whole alphabet and were thus able to
restore their knowledge completely.[9]

Even when we do not regress, ascending to higher levels
of spiritual consciousness makes us more sensitive to faults and
shortcomings we have learned to overlook. For these reasons, it
may be necessary to spend a lot of time working on one or several
stages of this spiritual growth scheme. Spiritual growth is a lifelong
process, so as long as we are committed to it, we will find
ourselves climbing this spiritual ladder many times, each time in a
new context, each time on a higher plane.

4
Submission:
Suppressing Anxiety

ANXIETY AND THE EGO

The first stage of therapy, as we said, is to suppress anxiety, that is, to deflate its significance. Although, theoretically, we could do this by directly downplaying the significance of the problem itself and demonstrating that things are not as bad as they seem, this is in most cases counter-productive. By the time a problem has become the cause of anxiety, the affected individual is already convinced of its extreme gravity. Trying to argue against this conviction will only compel him or her to prove how grave the problem really is.

The surer path is the roundabout one of reducing the magnitude of the problem by neutralizing the ego.[1] Although we may be tempted to think that anxiety results from a low self-image and that diminishing the ego would be adding insult to injury, this is far from the case. Obsession over an anxiety actually inflates the ego. It focuses us on ourselves so much that we may become incapable of relating to others.

Furthermore, ego spawns selfish desire, which in turn leads to worries. The greater we feel we are, the more we think we deserve; the more we think we deserve, the more we will be agitated by the lack of what we think we should have. The gulf between what we have and what we think we should have—or the way our life is and the way we think it should be—will disturb us continuously.

This syndrome is aptly illustrated by the story of "The Clever Man and the Simple Man"[2] told by the famed 18th century Hassidic master Rabbi Nachman of Breslov.[3]

Once, there were two friends, a simple man and a clever man. The simple man made the best of his lot, while the clever man was never satisfied with anything. Working as a goldsmith, he produced a perfect ring, but he suffered because the buyer did not appreciate it; on another occasion, when the buyer was happy, he suffered because he knew that there was a tiny flaw in the workmanship. He went from profession to profession, achieving higher levels of learning. He became a physician and then a philosopher, but was never content. His egocentricity—which was at the heart of his discontent—eventually led him to judge the whole world worthless and to question everything. As a result, he suffered constantly.

Then, the simple man and the clever man were summoned to an audience with the king. The simple man went happily and was elevated to a position at court. The clever man refused to go; by this point he had convinced himself that the king does not exist. In the end, he found himself in a "devil's pit" and only because of this most painful experience did he submit to the simple man's efforts to save him by faith and miracle. Ultimately, he was forced to look at the world again—to distinguish between reality and his own inner thoughts.

As we see in this story, the ego traps us in a self-perpetuating and self-augmenting spiral of anxiety. As our ego grows, so do our problems; as our problems worsen, our ego grows accordingly. To heal the psyche, we must neutralize the ego.

How, then, do we neutralize the ego? Here, again, there is a direct approach and an indirect approach. The direct approach is to begin by contemplating our own smallness; the indirect approach is to begin by contemplating the greatness of God.

> Rabbi Dovber of Mezritch was once asked by two of his disciples, Rabbi Elimelech of Lizhensk and Rabbi Zushya of Anipol, whether it is best to begin the process of self-refinement by contemplating the greatness of God or the smallness of man. Rabbi Dovber answered that in earlier generations it was possible (and preferable) to begin with the smallness of man, but in our times it is better to begin with the greatness of God.

In other words, the indirect approach is again the preferred one. If we begin by considering our own smallness, we may well succeed in convincing ourselves of it, but in the meantime we will still be focused on ourselves. Dwelling exclusively and persistently on our faults is likely to depress us and, as we have said, only serve to inflate the ego.

Once, however, we begin to contemplate the greatness of God, we can view our own smallness in the context of God's greatness, and thus deal with our own ego indirectly. Furthermore, inasmuch as our awareness of God's presence carries with it the awareness of His mercy, we will be spared feelings of dejection or depression when we examine our shortcomings.[4] The importance of the awareness of God's mercy cannot be overemphasized. We are allowed to examine our own shortcomings only in proportion to how conscious we are of God's mercy.

The sages of the Kabbalah were highly critical of melancholy, but at the same time, they did not advise us to ignore our faults in order to avoid feeling badly about them. Rather, they encouraged us to be constantly aware of God's infinite mercy and His continuous presence with us. In this way, we can face our faults fearlessly and securely, never falling into despair.

And just as the more we become aware of God's mercy, the more we can face our shortcomings objectively, so too, the more we face our shortcomings objectively, the more we become aware of God's mercy. Maintaining equilibrium between these two complimentary states of awareness is the basis of our relationship with God.

THE NATURE OF EXISTENCE: SUBMISSION WITHIN SUBMISSION

There are, of course, an infinite number of facets to "the greatness of God," for God is infinitely great in an infinite number of ways. The most comprehensive aspect of His greatness, however, is the absolute nature of His existence.

The fact that God created and continues to create the universe places the nature of His existence in direct contrast with the existence of everything else. For whereas everything else owes its existence to God, God's existence does not depend on anything else.

In terms of *absolute* reality, then, only God really exists. As the Torah proclaims, "there is nothing beside Him."[5] Everything else is part of a relative or dependent reality. If God were to stop willing some aspect of reality into existence, it would instantaneously cease to exist.

The logical conclusion of this line of thought is that nothing other than God is worthy of our esteem. This includes even the most exalted of God's creations—the human being. The absolute nature of God's existence implies the insignificance of humanity in comparison. If we dwell on God's infinity sufficiently, we will feel our own existence shrink in the face of His absolute reality. Without focusing on our ego directly, we will have delivered it a major blow, and when our ego is diminished, our worries are diminished accordingly. The awesome absoluteness and infinity of God make all our personal problems appear petty in comparison.

The feeling of smallness engendered by this way of thinking does not carry any negative implications for our self-image. This smallness is existential, a natural conclusion drawn from our awareness of the nature of our existence. This is just the way things are, and not our fault in any way: God is infinite and the human being is finite, and even the largest finite number imaginable is nothing compared to infinity.[6]

THE REALITY CHECK:
SEPARATION WITHIN SUBMISSION

Although meditating on the absolute nature of God's existence indeed delivers a major blow to the ego, it does not completely neutralize it. This is because the meditation we have described is too general to have such a profound effect. It attacks only the symptoms of the ego—the egocentric thoughts that give rise to anxiety—while the unconscious root of the ego itself remains fully entrenched and unaltered.

Indeed, if we meditate on any subject in only a general way, it will not have a profound or long-lasting effect. The lack of attention to detail leaves too much of our mind untouched and therefore unconvinced and unchanged. The mental structures we have grown accustomed to using are not affected by the broad brushstrokes painted by a general overview of a particular aspect of reality. Lack of attention to detail precludes an in-depth experience of Divine truth.

Only through detailed and thorough contemplation of some facet of Divine truth—with all its implications, ramifications, and applications—can we transcend our self-awareness and become entirely absorbed in the experience of this truth. Painstaking examination of the details, reflecting our sincere dedication to know the truth, brings us face to face with a clear, lucid perception of the truth's inner depth and essence. Thus, detailed contemplation enhances and even radically illuminates the awareness we gain by general contemplation.

Furthermore, when we contemplate a Divine truth in detail, we begin to adopt its inherent perspective on reality, to gradually rewire the circuitry of our mind according to our enlightened awareness. This forges new ways of thinking that will, in time, profoundly affect our emotional and behavioral responses to life.

Nonetheless, when we are suffering from some psychological malaise or anxiety, we are usually only capable at first of a general contemplation. Our preoccupation with our own problems does not allow us the peace or presence of mind to concentrate on the details of anything other than our own painful situation. We can meditate on other subjects in only a very broad way, focusing on overviews and immediate implications.

To realize this limitation is itself a humbling experience, for it awakens us to the extent to which our ego has crippled our capacities of perception and abstract thought. Without this humbling awareness, we would be apt to think that we have actually accomplished great things by rising above our own egocentricity somewhat. This, in itself, is just another trap of the ego.

Before the Ba'al Shem Tov passed away, his disciples asked him by what criteria they should choose a successor.

> He told them that they should ask each prospective candidate
> how to overcome the ego. If he offered a definitive antidote,
> this was a sure sign that he was not the one.[7]

General contemplation is therefore an admission of our ego's hold over us, which is an experience of submission. Within the overall process of submission, it is the first sub-phase, that of submission within submission.[8]

As we engage in this general form of contemplation, we will gradually be liberated from our limiting self-consciousness. We will then be ready to progress to a more detailed and deliberate meditation on the absolute reality of God and its implication in our lives. Since such detailed contemplation requires us to be detached from the constraints of our psychological problems, it is the second sub-phase of the overall process of submission: separation within submission.

Detailed contemplation of the absolute reality of God and the tenuous nature of creation means examining the implications, ramifications, and applications of these truths in all aspects of our lives. As the awareness of God's reality permeates our consciousness, we become increasingly aware of how much our lives—and life in general—contravene this awareness.

Furthermore, once we come to realize—even in a general way—that God is everything and we are insignificant in comparison, we are ready to consider that God has a plan and purpose for creation that supersedes any ideas we may have entertained as to what life and reality should be. God's ideals become the yardstick against which all is measured and evaluated. Sensing the implications of the absoluteness of God's reality, we begin to evaluate how our behavior measures up. Do we conduct our lives loving, fearing, and esteeming God, or a whole pantheon of lesser "deities"?

At some level, we all know that we possess an "animal soul," that is, a repository of selfish urges and drives. Although we generally like to identify ourselves with somewhat higher pursuits than these, a candid self-assessment will show that we unwittingly identify with the "animal soul" much of the time, that is, we consider its perspective and aspirations to be our own.

A rich man and a poor man were both invited to a sumptuous wedding feast. The poor man, who rarely had the opportunity to indulge in a good meal, devoured course after course with relish. The rich man ate the meal calmly and with detached nonchalance, for the wedding feast did not offer any fare that was substantially different than his daily meals.

The question is: who was more the prisoner of his physical drives? Even though the poor man seemingly lost control in the face of good food, the rich man indulged his lusts on a daily basis. Despite the nonchalant way he ate, his food-lust had become an ingrained part of his nature. If he would have been deprived of his daily fare, his lust for food would have surfaced and he would have demanded that it be satisfied. Thus, his physical drives were actually far more out of control than the poor man's. The poor man, even though he may have craved a delicious meal, had learned to live without it; he was not addicted.

While contemplating "the greatness of God" in general brings us to an awareness of our own insignificance, contemplating it in detail brings us further—to an awareness of our own baser drives. We come to realize that although we may put on a façade of propriety, we are no more refined than anyone else, and perhaps less refined than most.

Now we can examine our faults and shortcomings, which have been expressing themselves as our anxieties and fears. As we review them one by one, the absoluteness of our existential insignificance is driven home more and more graphically. Although we cannot—at least at this point—pinpoint the direct correlation between specific faults and specific anxieties, this process deals yet another blow to the ego.

Earlier, contemplating the infinity of God led us to the conclusion that creation is insignificant and does not possesses any independent existence. Now, however, when we contemplate our own shortcomings in all their graphic relief, we realize that not only do we not possess the intrinsic reality that God possesses, but that our present psychological state is, in fact, an *antithesis* of that reality.

Contrary to our earlier assumption that we are blameless victims of some malevolent force or circumstance, this realization leads us to the shocking but logical conclusion that we have only ourselves to blame for our anxieties. The darker side of our personality—those myriad instances of egoistic denial of God that we now realize dominate our consciousness—naturally surfaces as the psychological and/or physical malaises that we feel.

In this light, "victimization"—the temptation to see ourselves as victims of circumstance, family, or society—is essentially heresy. By taking victimization to its logical conclusion, we end up blaming God for everything or—if we cannot reconcile our suffering with the existence of a benevolent God—denying His existence. True, God runs the world and is therefore responsible for whatever unfortunate or fortunate circumstances we were born into. But this does not absolve us from personal responsibility.[9]

The sages teach that "the load matches the camel"[10] and "the reward is commensurate with the pain endured."[11] In other words, if Divine providence places us in a life-context that challenges us, this cannot serve as an excuse for surrendering or evading responsibility. God has His own way of balancing the books, and each one of us is judged in accordance with our

individual abilities and resources. Rather than saying, "Since my
life will never be the way it should be, it's no use trying," one
should say: "I have been given a challenge; let's see how well I can
overcome it and live my life."

Egocentricity and belief in God are thus mutually
exclusive. When egocentricity overtakes our consciousness, our
professed belief in God may be nothing other than a psychological
means of having someone to blame for whatever is going wrong in
our lives.

In contrast, contemplating "the greatness of God and the
smallness of man" has the opposite effect: we come to consider
the misfortunes Divine providence has dealt us to be hidden good,
since everything comes from God and everything God does is
good, for such is His nature. Our problems remain our own fault.
As the sages point out:

> Have you ever seen a wild beast or a bird with a
> profession? Yet they are sustained without
> anxiety. Now, they were created only to serve
> me [a human being], while I was created to serve
> God. Surely, then, I should make a living
> without anxiety! [The reason I do not is] because
> of my misdeeds, through which I have spoiled
> my livelihood.[12]

This realization roots out the ego even further, together
with the full spectrum of its anxieties. When we no longer feel that
we deserve anything, having less than we deserve cannot trouble
us. Detailed contemplation of the greatness of God leads us to
realize that the good He bestows on us is altogether undeserved.

Our response to undeserved Divine grace can only be unmitigated happiness and an upwelling of appreciation. Whereas egocentric people consider the good in their lives insufficient and are never satisfied with what they have, humble people consider the good in their lives to be above and beyond what they deserve. They are always "happy with their portion."[13] The more humble we are, the more undeserving we will consider ourselves, and the happier will we be with whatever God gives us.

When someone asked Rabbi Dovber of Mezritch how we can serve God with joy even while we are suffering, he directed him to his disciple, Rabbi Zushya of Anipol.[14] Now, it was well known that Rabbi Zushya was impoverished and well acquainted with suffering. Yet, when posed the question, Rabbi Zushya answered, "I don't know why the *Rebbe* sent you to me; I have known no suffering my whole life."

At another time Rabbi Zushya was asked: "How can you recite the daily morning blessing, 'Blessed are You, God, who has provided for all my needs,' when you know that your needs are not being met?" He answered: "For me, poverty is a need."

Rabbi Zushya was ever mindful of God's omnipresence and infinite goodness and mercy throughout his self-scrutiny. His trust in God kept him from feeling trapped by his problems and from falling into depression or despair.

The holiest day of the Jewish year is Yom Kippur, the day of atonement and forgiveness. On Yom Kippur, Jews fast and spend the day in the synagogue praying. The special liturgy of this day is replete with confessions and petitions for forgiveness. The intensity of feeling mounts throughout the day, reaching its climax at the closing service, *Ne'ilah*—literally, "locking"—when the final petitions are offered before the gates of forgiveness are locked.

But, as the Hassidic elder and counselor, Rabbi Mendel Futerfass[15] once rhetorically asked: Are we to assume that God wants us to spend the holiest day of the year focused on our sins? What sort of spiritual energy would be generated by a hall full of people focused on sin? Rather, the intention is that we focus on God, His infinite greatness, and His infinite goodness and mercy toward us. The final prayer is not called *Ne'ilah* because the gates of forgiveness are being locked, but because by this time we have so intensified our relationship with God and feel so close to Him that each of us experiences himself or herself alone with God, as though everyone else has, so to speak, been locked out of the room.

Why, then, all the confessions and petitions for forgiveness? Because, Rabbi Futerfass concluded, they are the truest expression of this closeness. Only when we feel truly close to someone who really means something to us do we realize how much there is to apologize for.

HEARTFELT PRAYER: SWEETENING WITHIN SUBMISSION

After intensive contemplation of our shortcomings, we turn to our Creator in prayer to bridge the chasm that separates us from Him. Crying out from the depths of our heart, we beseech God to bring us close to Him. Every feeling of distance from Him becomes the subject of another prayer, another cry directed toward Him.[16] As King David advises: "Cast your burden on God and He will sustain you."[17]

This type of prayer is not born of despair or depression, but rather of the self-disappointment that comes with humility. Although, as we said above,[18] being aware of our own smallness in the context of God's greatness makes us happy and confident, this happiness does not blind us to the necessity for self-improvement. On the contrary, the more we feel God's concern in our lives, the more we are driven to live up to our innate potential and not betray the Divine image within us.

In other words, although we are happy, we are also sad—or, as Rabbi Shneur Zalman of Liadi put it, "bitter."[19] This bitterness is a deep, existential dissatisfaction with life, due to our own shortcomings. If we are angry, we are not angry at the world, but with ourselves. "Bitterness" is the middle path between the resignation of self-acceptance (that absolves us from self-improvement) and the depression that comes from despairing of ever bettering ourselves. We have not given up on ourselves, but neither are we happy with the way we are. This is the "bitterness" that motivates us to pray.

It is a given in Judaism that when we are beset with problems—and that includes the problem of anxiety over life's difficulties—we should beseech God to help us solve them. Belief in God's omnipotence and mercy implies that He alone can and will provide the surest solution. Whether through the inspiring words of the psalms or the prayer book, or through spontaneous, informal verbalization of our heart's desires, we always seek God's benevolent involvement.[20]

We should never fall into the trap of thinking that since God is compassionate by nature there is no need for us to pray, or that, if God is making us suffer despite His compassion, it must be for our own good. Although it is certainly true that God is compassionate and everything He does is for our good, He also wants us to acknowledge our powerlessness before Him and be aware that we can and must turn to Him for everything. Even if our suffering is an atonement for our wrongdoing or a rectification of a previous incarnation, the sentence can always be commuted through heartfelt prayer.

The sages teach[21] that the reason the patriarchs and matriarchs were childless for so long was so that they would be inspired to beseech God on this account. Their need led them to pour out their hearts to God and thus build a relationship with Him.

> One cold, winter night, the Ba'al Shem Tov and his entourage paid an unannounced and incognito visit to a certain poor Jew.
> The peasant was overjoyed to fulfill the commandment of hospitality and welcomed his guests graciously. He ran to the forest to fetch wood to chop in order to serve them a hot drink, trekked into town to buy milk for their tea, gave them his family's sheets and pillows to sleep on, and served them the best meal he could afford. But the Ba'al Shem Tov and his disciples stayed for five days, eating him out of house and home! The peasant had to sell almost everything he owned in order to satisfy his guests' needs and demands.
> All the while, the peasant was grateful for the opportunity to host his guests. But that did not change the fact that as poor as he was before the Ba'al Shem Tov's visit, he was destitute by the time he left. When his children cried from hunger, he asked God why He had blessed him with the opportunity to host guests and had then left him bereft of the means to feed his family.
> Just then, a non-Jew knocked on the peasant's door and asked for a drink. The non-Jew eventually involved the peasant in business dealings that made the peasant wealthy.
> Later, the rich peasant later paid the Ba'al Shem Tov a visit. The Ba'al Shem Tov told him, "I saw that it was decreed in heaven that you should become rich, but the wealth could not come to you because you never asked for it. You were content with so little. Therefore, I had to eat you out of house and home so you would pray and ask for the bounty that was rightfully yours."[22]

By invoking God's mercy in prayer, we are admitting that certain things in life are just too big for us and we do not hold the keys to our own salvation. In so doing, we finally neutralize the ego, and when the ego is neutralized, its anxieties are neutralized together with it.

Heartfelt and humble prayer to God—our private conversation with our Creator—is the sweetening stage of submission before God. Having relinquished our delusions of self-reliance, we can know the sweetness of God's presence, mercy, and support.

As we will see, the simple act of articulating our problems aids the process of healing and resolution. Furthermore, our reliance on God's goodness and mercy assures us that our prayers will be speedily answered.

This assurance is, in fact, reflected in the liturgy. The central part of the silent prayer (the *Amidah*) is a series of requests for specific spiritual and material needs, each request followed by a blessing praising God for fulfilling it. Since Jewish law forbids uttering blessings in vain, this liturgical pattern implies that God is ready to grant our requests whenever we sincerely pray that He do so. If it seems to us that all our prayers are not immediately answered, it is because we have fallen back into our old, egoistic ways and have blocked the channels of Divine beneficence before God's answer has had a chance to materialize.[23]

In summary, we have examined the following threefold process of submission (suppressing anxiety):

	3. sweetening within submission	Heartfelt and humble prayer to God
suppressing anxiety	2. separation within submission	Detailed contemplation of the greatness of God; awareness of one's baser drives
	1. submission within submission	General contemplation of the greatness of God; awareness of the insignificance of this world in general and oneself in particular

5
Separation:
Ignoring Anxiety

OBJECTIVITY

Once we have reduced the immensity of the anxieties, problems, or dark thoughts that plague us by suppressing them and subduing our ego, we can proceed to the next phase of therapy, actively ignoring them.

This intermediate phase of therapy is an essential prerequisite for the final phase—articulating the problem— through which we heal the unhealthy situation or frame of mind altogether. This is because in order to relate to something objectively and analyze it truthfully, we must first be released from our subjective ties to it.

Ignoring anxiety is predicated on the assumption that the essence of the Divine soul is unaffected by the weaknesses of the animal soul, and it is therefore possible to rectify our problems by bringing our Divine side to the fore, enabling it to assume full reign over our personality.

Since conventional psychology does not generally speak of—nor, for that matter, recognize—the existence of a Divine soul, it is only to be expected that many schools of psychology disapprove of the manner of dealing with the manifestations of the lower urges we are about to detail; they see these techniques as an evasion, a way of avoiding direct confrontation. We will examine the implications of attempting to bypass this phase of therapy later on.

Identifying with our Divine soul gives us an abstract vantage point in our mind from which we can relate impartially to the world and to our own problems and anxieties. When we feel detached from the world in this way—something of "a stranger in a strange land"[1]—we can view it objectively, see what needs to be rectified and begin to see how to rectify it. Without this detachment, we are trapped by the natural laws of the world. Indeed, our ability to rectify the world and transform it into a home for God depends on our ability to feel that we ourselves are not subject to the inherent constrictions of the world. Detachment is prerequisite to influence.

Thus, before we proceed to the stage of sweetening, wherein we transform God's concealment in this world into the Divine revelation it was meant to be, we must first pass through the stage of separation.

DISMISSING NEGATIVE THOUGHTS: SUBMISSION WITHIN SEPARATION

In everyday life, we constantly (and naturally) ignore anxiety—or potential sources of anxiety—by spontaneously dismissing most of the thoughts that surface from the subconscious. This is a healthy form of suppression that simply prevents every little negative urge or complex that comes to mind from derailing the normal functions of living. Often enough, these murmurings are not very deeply rooted in the subconscious and therefore do not warrant much attention. In these cases, ignoring the problem is indeed the best way to deal with it. As we have noted, unwarranted attention to a problem will only aggravate it and artificially exaggerate it.

More full-blown anxieties require conscious dismissal, a deliberate choice to ignore what presents itself as a burning issue. In this spirit, the sages teach that the best way to fight anger is to remain silent and the best way to deal with jealousy is to ignore it.[2]

Along with ignoring our problems—and especially if our dark thoughts do not leave us alone and we are unable to simply ignore them—we should turn heavenward and implore God for help. The fact that we are still beset by anxieties indicates that it was not enough—in this case, at least—to ask God to bring us closer to Him (the thrust of our prayers at the sweetening within submission stage). Here, we beseech God to save us from the dark thoughts that engulf us.

If our prayer is sincere and earnest enough, God will come to the rescue. The soul is the Divine dimension of the human being—as the Torah says, "God's people are a part of Him."[3] So, by beseeching God to rescue our soul, we are in effect calling upon Him to assist His own representative, a spark of His own essence, in its struggle to overcome the forces of evil. Since God has, so to speak, a vested interest in the spiritual success of every one of us in our struggle to conquer evil, He will save us for His own sake.[4]

The awareness that, as creations of God formed in His image, we are essentially good—and existentially separate from the problems and anxieties that beset us—implies that we can avail ourselves of His help at any time. God is always standing at our side,[5] ready to save us from the onslaught of dark thoughts that attack us. In this sense we can always consider ourselves above the misery of this world.

When we consciously choose to ignore a problem or appeal to God for help, we are admitting that confronting it ourselves would make matters worse. Realizing that we cannot deal with our problems directly prevents our ego from reasserting itself.

This admission of our inadequacy and our reliance on God is the sub-phase of submission within separation. At this point, we are not yet attempting a direct confrontation with darkness, nor are we even asking God for strength to combat it.

SELF-REDEFINITION: SEPARATION WITHIN SEPARATION

The next stage of therapy is positive self-redefinition. As we said previously, one of the dangers of anxiety is that it may encourage us to define ourselves in terms of our problems. We can counter this pitfall by becoming aware of our Divine soul, the undefiled point of inner purity that cannot be sullied by the illusions of the animal soul's ego and the anxieties it produces.

Despite the real or imagined gravity of our situation, there remains deep within us an untouched and unaffected point of wholeness and goodness. As soon as we remember this, we can use this point to recast our whole situation in a more positive light. Without this awareness, we may conceive of our inner selves as problematic or even tainted by some psychological disorder or complex. In truth, however, we possess an identity and selfhood that is independent of our anxieties. If we can gradually identify with this inner point of health, we can rehabilitate ourselves in its image.

Depression, for example, often springs from a deep sense of failure in life. Having failed repeatedly, depressed people start to give up.[6] Because they are unable to achieve their goals, they lose their motivation and become physically and morally weak. In extreme cases, they may even lose their will to live.

Such frustration and disappointment are the side effects of an unchecked ego. Frustrated or disappointed people feel how far away they are from their would-be self-image. Here, the destructive, ego-based feeling that one is nothing or worthless must be isolated from the constructive feeling that one is nothing in the presence of God.

R. is a young family man who does not seem to be able to hold down a job and provide for his wife and children. With no end in sight to the frustration and embarrassment this situation causes, he falls into depression. He is unable to identify anything good in his situation, and feels like a total failure.

In dealing with his depression, R. must begin the process of separation by addressing the question: "Is it good to be nothing or is it bad to be nothing?" Clearly, his present feeling of worthlessness is negative, but he must be made aware that the feeling of being nothing can also exist in a positive context. The initial, unrectified feeling of nothingness is in fact a mixture of two antithetical psychological states. It is good to feel that one is nothing in the presence of the infinite, all-encompassing being of God; it is bad to feel that one is nothing in *any* other context. R. must choose the positive nothingness and reject the negative nothingness. In this way, he will lift himself out of his depression, and learn to identify with his Divine soul, his true, intrinsic worth.

In this context, R. can be taught to think of his present state of failure as a blessing in disguise. He can learn to conceive of the life-process he is undergoing as that of a seed that must decompose in the ground in order to sprout. He should meditate daily on God's continual recreation of the world *ex nihilo*—"out of *nothing*"—in order to realize how

being nothing can lead to becoming something truly
worthwhile. If he can enter the positive state of
"nothingness," the success in life he never thought possible
may ensue.

The most effective way of contacting this inner point of
origin is meditative prayer. Normally, our instinctive awareness of
being rooted in a higher, spiritual source is buried deep within our
unconscious. We can, however, bring it into our conscious mind
through meditative prayer.

Since we are seeking here to renew ourselves in our Divine
origin, an abstract attempt to visualize ourselves ascending to our
spiritual root will not work, for this is too superficial. Rather, the
ascent must be part and parcel of our deepest, heartfelt prayer to
God. We meditate in God's presence, asking Him to elevate us and
draw us near to Him, our ultimate source.

Rabbi Dovber of Mezritch was once visited by an old
friend who was a learned Kabbalist. This friend spent the
whole year studying the Torah, but took off two weeks each
year to travel to the fair in Leipzig to earn his living. Noting
how much time Rabbi Dovber spent in his prayers, his friend
remarked that he, too, prayed according to the meditative
system of the famed mystic, Rabbi Isaac Luria (the "Ari"), but it
did not take him so much time.

Rabbi Dovber asked him, "When you go to the fair in
Leipzig, you have to make your arrangements, pack up your
merchandise, embark on the trip, check into an inn, sell your
wares, pack up whatever is left, and finally make the trip back
home. This takes you away from your beloved study of the
Torah for several weeks. Wouldn't it save time if you just
pictured yourself going through all those steps in the comfort
of your own home?"

"Surely," the friend answered, "there is a difference
between visualizing something happening in the mind and
actually doing it! Actually going there takes much more time,
but it is real."

"That," Rabbi Dovber answered, "is why it takes me so much longer to pray than it takes you, even though we follow the same meditations."

The literature of Kabbalah describes how the progressive sections of the liturgy are an ascent to and descent from this Divine awareness. As we advance through the liturgy, we ascend through corresponding stages of Divine awareness and self-effacement until we reach total absorption in the reality of God. We then gradually descend back into awareness of the world and ourselves with renewed inspiration and dedication.[7]

Meditative prayer thus goes beyond asking God to fulfill our needs. Although that is a proper, elementary aspect of prayer, our intent in meditative prayer is to link our soul to God. We accomplish this by meditating on Divinity and the origin of our soul within it.

In truth, this "return to roots" is an essential facet of human psychology, as evidenced by the popularity of genealogy research, ethnic consciousness, nationalism, and so on. All these phenomena are expressions of the soul's instinctive drive to renew itself at its spiritual origin. Indeed, according to Kabbalah, every element of creation has its higher spiritual origin to which it is capable of ascending through meditation.[8] The most familiar example of a creature instinctively returning to its physical source is that of salmon swimming upstream to their native freshwater habitats in order to reproduce. The Midrash teaches that the entire animal, vegetable, and mineral kingdoms "sing" constantly, that is, "meditate on" and experience their Divine origins.[9] One of the missions of the Jewish people is to awaken this latent consciousness in all of creation.

Thus, through meditative prayer, the soul acquires the wings of consciousness necessary to rise above and beyond the confines of the physical lower self with its milieu of negative thoughts and anxieties and connect with its spiritual higher self, its soul-root.

We cannot focus on Divinity, however, if we are weighed down by worldly worries. Emptying the mind of all disturbing thoughts is thus a prerequisite to this type of prayer.[10]

As we climb the ladder of meditative prayer, we become increasingly aware of our insignificance in the presence of God. This, in turn, increases our experience of His mercy. Feeling His mercy restores our confidence—this time not as an expression of our ego but of our reliance on His support—filling our heart with hope and initiative. With God at our side, we are no longer "nothing": we can assert ourselves; we can take action.

The Torah teaches us that we must first reject evil and only then focus on the good.[11] By rejecting the negative feeling of nothingness, we can attain initiative to act with self-confidence.

Nevertheless, this self-confidence must be balanced. Together with our self-confidence, we must nullify our sense of self-accomplishment and recognize that all credit belongs to God. We must never forget that without God's help, we are indeed total failures. In other words, we must nurture our positive feeling that we *are* nothing. Our positive sense of self must be balanced by a concomitant sense of selflessness.[12]

POSITIVE THINKING:
SWEETENING WITHIN SEPARATION

The next stage of separation is to *actively* ignore anxieties by replacing dark, negative thoughts with "sweet," positive ones. This most fundamental, straightforward remedy for worries and troubles is encapsulated in the Hassidic saying: "Think good, and it will be good."[13]

Although we cannot stop thinking, we can choose what to think about. Left to its own devices, the mind will tend to fill itself with negative thoughts that spring from its unrectified subconscious. It is therefore necessary to consciously occupy the mind with alternatives. Filling it with positive thoughts is the surest way to avoid falling into depression or despair.

Any positive thought will help dispel the darkness of negativity, but contemplating ideas from the Torah—particularly those that engender feelings of holiness, optimism, and happiness—is especially effective in this regard.[14] As King David states: "The precepts of God are straightforward, gladdening the heart."[15]

The image that best describes this technique is found in the story of Joseph and his brothers. When Jacob sent Joseph to check on his brothers well-being, they threw him into a pit, where he remained while they debated how to get rid of him. The Torah relates that "the pit was empty; there was no water in it."[16] The Midrash notes this apparent redundancy and explains its implication: the pit was indeed empty of water, but it was filled with snakes and scorpions.[17] Because Joseph was a good and holy man, these creatures did not harm him.

Water is understood in the Talmud[18] to symbolize the life-giving and refreshing flow of the Torah's wisdom. The pit represents the human mind, which ideally is meant to be a vessel for holding the water of the Torah. The snakes and scorpions represent the negative, destructive thoughts that overtake the mind in the absence of positive, Torah-oriented thoughts. Joseph represents the ability of the mind to transform negative thoughts into positive thoughts. He neutralized the power of the negative forces that had overrun the pit so they could not harm him.

We all have our inner Joseph—the ability to replace our negative thoughts with positive ones. If we are able to call upon and utilize this inner ability, so much the better; if not, we should seek the inspiration to reorient our perspective from those who have. Every generation has its Joseph, the "righteous one, [who is] the foundation of the world."[19] By seeking his counsel—whether in person or by studying his teachings—we can awaken the inner Joseph latent in our own souls and access our inner power to think positively.

Besides safeguarding us from negativity, positive thinking about the specific problem troubling us can actually influence the course of events for the better.[20] The power of positive thinking to bring about good and of negative thinking to bring about evil is well known; indeed, it is the essence of cognitive psychotherapy.

We may choose whether we react optimistically or pessimistically to any given situation. The objective facts are the same, but the way we respond to them is our choice, as the Torah tells us, "I call upon heaven and earth to witness before you this day: life and death I have placed before you, blessing and curse; therefore, choose life…"[21]—choose to be optimistic. We should certainly utilize this potent tool to improve the quality of our life in general and our mental well-being in particular.[22]

Here again, the power of optimism to positively influence the course of events is enhanced by contemplating ideas from the Torah. Diverting the mind from a problem by immersing it in the study of the Torah may seem like a form of escapism, since the problem remains unsolved and we are only postponing dealing with it. The effectiveness of this technique, however, lies in the fact that the Torah connects us with God, its source. The essential goodness of the Torah endows our positive thinking with more power than it possesses otherwise.

The Torah—being God's wisdom—is also the source of the solutions to all problems, and by studying it we can access the solutions it offers. The Ba'al Shem Tov teaches that whoever studies the Torah for its own sake will be privileged to always see its relevance to his or her personal life.[23]

In order to integrate this power inherent in the Torah, we must first recognize and contact our soul-root in Divinity, for "the Torah and God are one."[24] We do this through meditative prayer, as described above.[25] After ascending to the heights of Divine consciousness, we are inspired to fill our lives with this newly-acquired enlightenment, which we do by studying the Torah, God's self-revelation in this world. Filling our consciousness with Torah grants us the spiritual power necessary to subsequently face our problem with optimism, confidence, and the insight to know how to deal with it.

The classic illustration of the power of positive thinking is the following incident from the life of Rabbi Akiva, the illustrious sage who was martyred by the Romans.

Rabbi Akiva was once traveling. He came to a town where he hoped to find a place to stay, but he was refused lodging everywhere. Nonetheless, he said, "Whatever God does is for the good," and spent the night in an open field.

He had with him a rooster to wake him up, a donkey to carry his belongings, and a lamp to study by. But the wind blew out the lamp, a weasel killed the rooster, and a lion devoured the donkey. Yet he said again, "Whatever God does is for the good."

In the morning, when he went into town, he learned that during the night a band of Roman soldiers had come and carried away its inhabitants. He had been spared because the Romans had been unaware of his presence. Had the lamp not been blown out, they would have seen it and gone after him. Had the rooster crowed or the donkey brayed, they would have heard and captured him. Realizing this, he said, "Did I not say that whatever God does is for the good?!"[26]

Rabbi Akiva's ability to perceive all that happened to him optimistically derived ultimately from his devoted immersion in the study of the Torah.[27]

In summary, we have examined the following threefold process of separation (ignoring anxiety):

ignoring anxiety	3. sweetening within separation	thinking positive thoughts; active optimism
	2. separation within separation	meditative prayer; consciousness of being "above" the world
	1. submission within separation	dismissing negative thoughts; admission of inability to confront evil directly

6
Sweetening:
Articulating Anxiety

THE ROLE OF THE COUNSELOR

Having negotiated the preparatory stages of submission and separation, we may now proceed to the concluding stage of therapy, sweetening. It is here that the role of the counselor, mentor, or therapist comes into full play.

The separation stage (passively and actively ignoring anxiety) provides the objectivity necessary for us to safely explore the deep crevices of our personality—even the dark, unpleasant ones—in order to uncover the roots of our negative thoughts and anxieties and consciously deal with them. We have been silent and have severed ourselves from evil; now it is time for us to speak.

We should begin this verbal excavation process privately, by exploring the dark caverns of our soul with our Creator. When ready, we should articulate our anxieties to a counselor—a good friend, a trusted therapist, or a spiritual mentor—who can hear our troubles and objectively advise us how to deal with them.

Articulating our anxieties to another person elicits, in the words of King Solomon quoted earlier, "a good word" which will turn our problems "into joy." This "good word" offered by the counselor may be some sound advice or some deep way of understanding the root of the problem. As we shall see, articulation and dialogue with another contributes to the healing process in three ways.

THE NEED FOR ANOTHER: SUBMISSION WITHIN SWEETENING

First of all, simply articulating the problem to someone else sweetens it to a certain degree. When our ideas are denied expression, our basic human drive to enhance life is frustrated. If we have a positive idea, we want to express it in order to contribute to our own or others' well-being; if we have a problem, we want to air it in the hope that someone can help us resolve it. Talking is pleasurable because it releases this tension.[1] The pleasure of self-expression reciprocally sweetens whatever we are talking about. Even if we are articulating a problem, the promise of resolution that is inherent in the articulation softens its edge and allows us a foretaste of the anticipated remedy.

By articulating our problems, we also demonstrate to ourselves that as deep and complex as our problems may be, it is nonetheless possible to express them, and if it is possible to express them, it will ultimately be possible to resolve them. Articulation also helps us focus and define our problems. This is a major step toward their resolution, for knowing the malaise is half the cure.[2]

Furthermore, the experience of talking teaches us—even if subliminally—that we are not alone in life, but are enveloped by God's presence and mercy. Talking implies a listener, and the most sensitive and understanding listener is, of course, God Himself.

The innate human urge to articulate, no matter to whom, may thus be perceived as an unconscious expression of our faith in God's unconditional willingness to hear us.[3] This awareness of God's mercy provides further solace and comfort to the ailing soul, for it allows us to remain close and connected to Him despite our shortcomings.

The counselor can assist us in all the previous stages of therapy. He can help us meditate on the absolute reality of God, feel God's presence and mercy supporting us, evaluate our lives, coach us in ignoring our anxieties, and teach us the arts of petitionary and meditative prayer and positive thinking. Here, the pleasure of release can be facilitated by the counselor's reassurance that the deep difficulties we have uncovered are not a threat to our relationship with God.

By articulating our anxieties, we demonstrate that we are dependent on other people (or God) to help us deal with them. This phase of therapy is thus a humbling experience, one of submission.

THE LOCAL SOLUTION: SEPARATION WITHIN SWEETENING

The fact that the counselor is not suffering from the same problem we are suffering from enables him to see it from a different vantage point. If the problem is not too complex, the counselor's objective perspective may well be all that is needed to solve it.

If not, this is where the counselor engages us in dialog so that together we may uncover the most effective solution. Since we have already dissociated ourselves from our suffering, we can be open to our counselor's advice. Since we see ourselves standing above our situation, we can objectively examine our options for a resolution. Although the counselor's recommendation may not be the one that we ultimately adopt, it starts the process of dialogue.

E. believes that no one will like her unless she loses weight. Failing to lose weight, she is overtaken with anxiety. Her depressed feelings and loss of positive self-image prevent her from functioning in the wholesome, cheerful way every person should. Because her attitude does not encourage people to like her, her anxiety becomes a self-fulfilling prophecy. Seeing that she is not well-liked, she sinks into depression and lethargy, seeks respite in food, and shuns exercise. This causes her to gain more weight, and so the cycle continues.

Obviously, one "solution" to E.'s problem is to stop overeating. There are all kinds of techniques she could use to get herself to do this, and if one works, she will lose weight and consider herself suddenly "likeable." Her attitude toward herself will rub off on others, and people will begin to like her again.

So, the problem has been solved—or has it? Is there any guarantee that E. will ever lose enough weight to consider herself "likeable," or, if she does win the war against weight, that she won't overdo it and risk becoming anorexic? Has E. changed in any way that will prevent her from gaining weight in the future, or from replacing her weight-myth with some other reason not to be liked?

For all these reasons, the simple "solution," reducing her food intake, is not a real solution at all.

To overcome this problem, E. must transcend the rigid mode of thinking in which she is trapped. This is not to say that she has to deny her pursuit of good health and a comely appearance, but rather that she has to deny that being overweight precludes being well liked. E.'s counselor must help her stand up to years of overt and covert indoctrination in shallow values and summon from within her the courage to behead this internalized dragon.

E. must come to understand that being liked is a function of an individual's attitude toward herself and toward others: if she exudes likeability, she will be liked; if she learns to value and develop her points of inner worth rather than be

> obsessed with her external shell, others will respond to her accordingly. She must know that "even if I do not lose weight, I can still be liked; it's up to me to be likeable." In her daily confrontation with the symbols and attitudes of our materialistic culture, sustaining this affirmation will take a great deal of courage and stamina, and require her to repeatedly and consistently remind herself of her new, higher perspective on life.
>
> As to her weight problem, the counselor can help E. realize that if, by Divine providence, she is overweight right now, there must be a positive purpose in it. For example, she can come to realize that the discipline and self-control she will have to learn in order to return to her proper weight will build her character and benefit her in other areas of her life.

Here, the counselor helped E. rise to a higher level of perception, where what was originally perceived as a mutual exclusivity (being overweight and well-liked) becomes entirely plausible. The same is true for many other dilemmas; by helping us rise to a higher level of perception, the counselor can show us how a bind we find ourselves in is often just a result of our own limited conception of things.[4]

This is the "good word" that King Solomon promises us will "gladden" our hearts when we suppress, ignore, and finally articulate our anxieties.

The type solution we have described here relates only to the level of the psychological wound that has surfaced in the consciousness of the suffering person. To borrow the terminology of modern physics, this is a "local" solution. The next phase of therapy is to find the "non-local" solution, which tackles the root of the psychological condition, transforming this evil into good.

TRANSFORMING EVIL INTO GOOD:
SWEETENING WITHIN SWEETENING

The deepest form of help the counselor can offer is to help us come to view the root of our problem in a positive light. This radical turnabout is the culmination of the entire therapeutic process and may be considered the quintessence of the Kabbalistic approach to psychotherapeutic healing. This final sweetening occurs when we reach a new, insightful perception of reality necessitated by the existence of the specific problem. This new perception enables us to understand the real, inner flaw that led to the problem in the first place and with this new knowledge adjust our orientation to life so that we will no longer fall into the same trap. Though born of the tension created by the problem, this new perception of reality focuses on something much bigger: the root of the problem, the inconsistent, immature perception of reality that allowed the problem to exist and develop.[5]

All along, we have seen how some redeeming factor can be found in any problem, how every cloud has a silver lining. Here, we are asserting that the problem itself, when properly reinterpreted, is the key to redemption—that the cloud *itself*, or at least part of it, is silver.

Positive reinterpretation of the problem is based on the Kabbalistic view of evil and the Ba'al Shem Tov's perspective on Divine providence.

We are taught in Kabbalah that for anything to exist, including the worst evil, there must be a spark Divine energy, an element of God's will, within it. In the case of evil, this Divine spark is obviously hidden, since the very reality of evil is the denial of God or His will. In the imagery of the Kabbalah, the spark is likened to a "kernel" or "fruit" held captive within the evil "shell" or "peel." By rejecting the evil, we reveal the inner Divine spark enlivening it. We break the shell and liberate the spark.

But we can do more than just reject the evil and break the shell. Through positive reinterpretation, we can utilize the liberated spark of goodness to transform whatever is possible of the evil context itself into good. Metaphorically speaking, part of the shell/peel is edible, and may even contain nutrients not contained in the kernel/fruit itself. Whatever evil cannot be transformed into good is annihilated; without the energy of its Divine spark, it cannot continue to exist.

The *Zohar*, the classic text of the Kabbalah, illustrates this dual nature of evil with the following parable:[6]

> A king had an only son whom he dearly loved. He therefore warned him not to be enticed by immoral women, and told him that anyone so defiled was not worthy to enter the royal palace. The son lovingly promised to abide by his father's will.
>
> Now, outside the palace there lived a beautiful prostitute. After a while, the king thought: "Let me see how devoted my son is to me." So he sent for the woman and told her, "Go seduce my son, for I wish to test his devotion to me." She proceeded to pursue the prince and tried her best to lure him. The son, however, obeyed his father's command and refused all her advances. This made the father rejoice greatly. Bringing his son into the innermost chambers of his palace, he showered

many gifts and treasures on him and gave him
great honor.

Who caused the prince to receive all this
honor? The prostitute! Is she then to be praised
or blamed? She is surely to be praised, for she
fulfilled the king's command, caused the son to
receive gifts and treasures, and deepened the
father's love for his son.

When the prince rejects the overtures of the prostitute in
devotion to his father, two things happen. First, it is revealed that
the prostitute, who was previously regarded as a criminal,
possesses an inner point of desire to serve the king and obey his
word. This revelation is the liberation of the Divine spark held
captive in the shell of the prostitute. Second, the prostitute's talent
to seduce has been employed for the good, to fulfill the king's
command. The shell itself has been transformed into good.

Thus, there is a core of good in all that is bad. Once we
identify this core, we can use it to enhance our spirituality and
heighten our awareness of God.

From this higher perspective, the darkness inherent in evil
is seen to be both illusion and reality. Only the illusion must be
totally denied, while the dark reality inherent in evil, the potent
nutrients contained in the shell, may be redeemed. This process is
described in the *Zohar* as "transforming darkness into light and
bitterness into sweetness."[7]

Divine providence, the fact that God oversees and guides
the affairs of creation, is a basic tenet of Judaism. The Ba'al Shem
Tov taught that Divine providence extends even to a leaf falling
from a tree in a forest, determining when and in what direction it
will fall, and that this seemingly insignificant event affects all of

reality and brings the world closer to its ultimate rectification. Today, we would say that God oversees and directs everything down to the smallest subatomic particle or force that exists.

This does not mean that we do not possess free choice. We are free agents and must assume full responsibility for our actions.

Throughout the ages, theologians have tried to resolve the mutual exclusivity of the doctrines of Divine providence and free will. The ultimate solution is that for our finite minds there is no logical solution: the two doctrines constitute a theological paradox. The way we live out the paradox, however, is clear. We invoke Divine providence in making sense of the past and we invoke free choice in facing the future. God, as it were, removes His providence with regard to the choices we make, but after we have made them, it becomes retroactively revealed that they were predestined parts of the great Divine plan.

Thus, whatever happens to us is directly attributable to God's providence, and since God is good and merciful, even if we find ourselves in a depressing psychological state, it, too, must be for our greater good.[8]

Moreover, it is taught in Hassidism that the good concealed in an apparently bad situation is actually of a higher order than good that can be readily recognized as such.[9] God sometimes chooses to be good to us in ways that seem bad to us because the good He wishes to bestow upon us in these cases is so intense that we would be unable to assimilate it otherwise. Like a precious commodity that must be wrapped in coarse material for its protection, the highest forms of good must sometimes be concealed in their apparent opposite.

Thus, rather than feeling that God is ignoring us or has abandoned us, we should learn to consider our suffering a personal gift from God, and one that in fact expresses His greatest love for us. And so it is written in the Book of Proverbs, "It is the one whom God loves that He rebukes."[10]

This is indeed a test of faith, and it is our counselor's job to help us deepen our faith in God, His unmitigated goodness, and His providence over all facets of life. When we succeed, we will have uncovered a more profound dimension of our personality than would have been otherwise manifest. Furthermore, we will have renewed our connection with God, and even deepened it, no longer limiting it by the parameters of good and evil as we initially perceived them.

Once we have successfully passed through all the preceding stages of the therapeutic process—that is, when we can look at our problem objectively, can identify ourselves with our inner essence of goodness rather than our anxieties, and have deepened our faith to the extent that we can experience our problems as a loving gift from God—we are ready to analyze our deepest psychological problems and transform their evil roots into good. The hesitations mentioned above about confronting the darker aspects of the subconscious no longer apply, since the groundwork has been laid for facing them constructively.

By undergoing the preceding, preparatory stages of the Kabbalistic process of psychotherapy, we become deeply conscious of God's infinite mercy enveloping us at all times. Only in this consciousness may we safely and objectively evaluate our own psychological health. Knowing we can fall back on His love, we are not afraid to face the truth about ourselves; we do not feel the need to hide behind excuses or justifications for our behavior.

It is for this reason that, according to the teachings of the Kabbalah, we should not confront the darker aspects of our personality that lie buried deep within our subconscious until we have attained an awareness of our inner Godliness. On the contrary: it is an act of God's mercy that the subconscious exists, so the darkness that "lurks in the hearts of men" can stay hidden until we are ready to face it.[11] God's ultimate plan, the reason He placed the darkness in our hearts in the first place, is that—when we are psychologically ready—we transform the potential energy latent in the darkness into the light of rectified consciousness and new life, as will be explained.

Our very readiness to confront our deep fears and anxieties further weakens their power over us. Our fearlessness in discussing them openly lays to rest our image of them as unassailable dragons that lurk in the dark undercurrents of our subconscious mind.

When we discover a local solution to our problem, we sweeten it in its own context. When we reach the root of the problem, identify it as an indivisible part of our entire existential state and transcend that state, we transform and sweeten our entire reality.

R., a young woman, is ready and desires to marry, but she is anxious over her failure so far to find her true soul-mate. She has begun to fear that she may never get married, and her obsession with this fear is taking its toll on her ability to live life normally. Common sense would tell her to widen her circle of connections, improve her appearance, or the like. On the spiritual plane, one may advise her to pray to God, give charity, etc. Although this type of advice certainly might help, it does not address her underlying fear of not getting married.

Although R.'s counselor could attempt to deal with her psychological problem "locally" by sweetening her underlying fear of never marrying, the gravity of marriage and its implications for her future call for a deeper, "non-local" solution. In the course of their dialogue, R.'s counselor explains to her that the reason she has not found her soul-mate yet is that God wants her to find her own true way in life first. Marrying before she clarifies her life-goals and objectives would likely not work out well for her. Although she feels ready to marry, and on some level indeed is, God, in

His love for her and desire that she fulfill her true potential in
life, knows that she is, in truth, not ready yet.

When she succeeds in clarifying her life's direction, things
will begin to fall into place by themselves. She will meet new
friends, be introduced to a different type of man, and, with
the help of God, merit to find her true soul-mate and get
married.

This is a classic example of a "non-local" solution. With
the recognition of Divine providence—"it is because of God in
His love for me that I am not yet married"—the "real" evil of
being unmarried has been transformed into good. As well, the
illusion that "I will never marry" has vanished.

Positive reinterpretation is the ultimate goal of the entire
therapeutic process: to bare the hidden evil and transform it into
good. Each successive stage of the therapeutic process takes us to
a further state of readiness to defy the root of our inner evil and
sweeten it.

The preceding techniques of suppressing, ignoring, and
sweetening anxiety are certainly safer in that they avoid unlocking
the closet and looking the monster in the face, but they are less a
test of the strength of our own inner goodness. When we are not
challenged by the dark forces, we do not have to tap the inner core
of goodness within us; it therefore remains latent. In this final
stage, we reveal the power of our inner goodness to reverse
psychological inertia and fundamentally change the way we live
life.

In summary, we have examined the following threefold
process of sweetening (articulating anxiety):

articulating anxiety	3. sweetening within sweetening	seeing the good in the root of the evil; transforming the root of the evil into good
	2. separation within sweetening	awareness of the inner core of goodness; advice for directly dealing with the evil
	1. submission within sweetening	release of tension by articulating the problem; objectivity

We may now summarize the full picture of the entire therapeutic process:

3. sweetening (speech)	articulating anxiety	sweetening within sweetening	seeing the good in the root of evil; transforming the root of evil into good
		separation within sweetening	awareness of inner core of goodness; advice for directly dealing with evil
		submission within sweetening	release of tension through articulation of the problem; objectivity
2. separation (severing)	ignoring anxiety	sweetening within separation	thinking positive thoughts; active optimism
		separation within separation	meditative prayer; consciousness of one's soul being rooted above the world
		submission within separation	dismissing negative thoughts; admission of inability to confront evil directly
1. submission (silence)	suppressing anxiety	sweetening within submission	heartfelt and humble prayer to God
		separation within submission	detailed contemplation of the greatness of God; awareness of one's baser drives
		submission within submission	general contemplation of the greatness of God; awareness of the insignificance of this world in general and oneself in particular

7
Positive Reinterpretation and Inner Transformation

THE CHALLENGE

It seems that in our time, widespread familiarity with the concepts of modern psychology has turned us all into would-be experts in psychoanalyzing ourselves. In a sense, this is as it should be. Ours is the generation of the ultimate and final Redemption, which will signal the annihilation of evil and the transformation of its inner core into goodness. Therefore, we are now called upon to participate in this process, and have been given the power to do so. We must become experts in the transformation of evil into good, even the kind of evil that it was once better to suppress or ignore.

As history progresses, each generation is further removed from the giving of the Torah at Mt. Sinai and is therefore on a lower spiritual rung than the generation that preceded it. The immense Divine revelation that entered the collective consciousness of the Jewish people at Mt. Sinai has become more and more dilute with time. This has left us both progressively more susceptible to the inroads of darkness into our subconscious mind and progressively less capable of directly combating it, especially in its more subtle forms. Thus, we find ourselves today at the bottom of a protracted spiritual descent from the heights of the experience of Mt. Sinai, plagued by more inner darkness and anxieties than any previous generation. Accordingly, as history has proceeded, the emphasis in the process of self-refinement has gradually shifted from directly uprooting our inner evil (which we could once accomplish easily because we possessed less evil and were psychologically healthier to begin with) toward suppressing and ignoring it (since it became more and more entrenched within us and we were not healthy enough to battle it head on).

On the other hand, as the Divine revelation at Mt. Sinai recedes into the obscurity of ancient history, things that were formerly acknowledged as detrimental to body and soul have become accepted as healthy. Inasmuch as evil gives rise to anxiety, this lack of clarity leads to further confusion, frustration, and more anxiety. This fact alone makes it imperative to relate to evil directly and reveal its true nature.

Ever since the giving of the Torah at Mt. Sinai, the Jewish people have toiled relentlessly to elevate reality, and the rest of humanity has struggled to advance civilization. This has not been for naught. Although each generation is indeed spiritually lower than the preceding one, the accomplishments of the generations are cumulative. In this sense, as time progresses, the world as a whole has become closer to total rectification and increasingly ready to tackle and defeat evil.

Furthermore, the imminent dawn of redemption is awakening us to our higher and surer selves; we feel the power of the messianic era already coursing through our veins.[1] This call to power emboldens us to attempt to face evil in a way that previous generations were rightly reticent to attempt.[2]

And since we are capable of this, it becomes our responsibility, for the advent of the ultimate Redemption is dependent upon the release of all the sparks of good trapped within evil. Revealing the evil within us in order to transform it into good becomes not only our own best interest but also our sacred duty.

Treating Phobias

The courage and fearlessness that accompanies the messianic call to power enables us, first of all, to cope with the various fears or phobias that plague us. In truth, *any* fear other than the fear of God is a phobia, i.e., a neurotic state of exaggerated or misdirected fear. Any fear other than the fear of God gives rise to secondary fears, the fear of fear, the fear of fear of fear, and so on. Each successive state of fear strikes its roots deeper in the psyche's unconscious, ultimately giving rise to negative psychological consequences. Only the fear of God is positive in essence, and of it is said, "*Happy* is the man who fears continuously."[3]

When we are young, fear is useful, for it protects us from harm. The parent wisely teaches the child to be afraid of fire or of playing in the street, and uses the child's fear of punishment to discipline him. But as we mature, we learn how to discipline ourselves and not to be afraid of things but simply to be careful. We thus can reserve our true fear solely for God, for inasmuch as God is the ultimate possessor of power, He is the only one we should truly fear.

In other words, to the extent that we remain afraid of anything other than God, we remain children, stuck at an immature level of emotional development. The reverse is also true:

a child who outgrows his childhood fears can be an "adult" even while still a child.[4]

In his last words to his young son, the Ba'al Shem Tov's father, Rabbi Eliezer, told him, "Yisrolik, fear nothing and no one other than God Himself!" From that day on, the Ba'al Shem Tov feared nothing but God. He walked fearlessly in the depths of the forest at all hours of day and night, fearing no creature or force, whether spiritual or physical.[5]

The classic example of a phobia is paranoia. Paranoid people envision other human beings, animals, and sometimes even objects, as threats; they feel pursued. Paranoia is poignantly described in the Book of Proverbs: "The lazy man said: 'There is a lion outside; [if I go outside] I'll be murdered in the street!'"[6]

Like all other phobias, paranoia can be attributed to the lack of fear of God. The less we fear God, the more we fear others.[7]

The Ba'al Shem Tov taught that the Midrashic statement that God is continuously creating the world anew[8] should be the basis of our understanding of reality.[9] Everything that exists, the Midrash teaches, is just a reflection of a higher spiritual antecedent.[10] Applied to the concept of fear, this means that anything that induces fear in us is spiritually rooted in God's attribute of fear. Thus, all worldly fears stem from and are merely imperfect versions of the fear of God.

This being the case, we should ponder—both before and when we feel afraid—why we should be afraid of an external, fallen object of fear. Shouldn't we recognize the inner kernel of its essence and realize that God sent us this fear in order to remind us to reinforce our fear of Him?

To cure ourselves of exaggerated and misdirected fear, we must first reject it and forcibly break it. If a person suffers from paranoia, for example, he must "endanger" his life and step outside, saying to God: "Do with me as you like; I am in Your hands." If we firmly believe in God, we will fear nothing, not even death.

During the Stalinist era, Rabbi Yosef Yitzchak of Lubavitch[11] was interrogated by a Communist official who sought to intimidate him by brandishing a gun. "This toy makes people cooperate," he said. "Fear of it has opened many a mouth." Rabbi Yosef Yitzchak replied: "That toy frightens only someone who has but a single world [*this* world] and many gods [the many forces that act in nature], but not one who has one God and two worlds [*this* world and the World to Come]." Stunned by the Rabbi's response, the Communist official put down his gun.[12]

By rejecting the fear as it first appears, one reveals its inner, Divine life force, the Divine attribute of fear that brings it into being.

But the fear of God is more than fear. In truth, it is a state of *awe*, an awareness of always standing in His presence. In order to truly stand in awe of God, we must not only *overcome* all other fears but actually *transform* them into the awe of God.[13] Transforming all other fears into the awe of God is a process of sweetening. When we do this, we experience a deep sense of liberation, release, and joy.[14]

We see here that treating fears and phobias is itself a threefold process of spiritual growth that follows the Ba'al Shem Tov's paradigm. Recognizing that God is the source of all power is an act of submission to His omnipotence. Fearing Him alone is an act of separating this fear from all spurious fears. Transforming all other fears into the fear of God is an act of sweetening them.

To summarize:

3. sweetening	transforming other fears into the fear of God
2. separation	fearing God alone
1. submission	realizing God's omnipotence

THE CONTEXT OF POSITIVE REINTERPRETATION

Together with knowing that we can stand up to the challenge of our times, to transform evil into good, we must also know that most of us can effect this transformation only by first conditioning ourselves to do so during counseling sessions and not when confronted with the challenge unprepared, in moments of trial. This is because it is very difficult to transform negativity into positivity on the spot, and indeed, Hassidic doctrine teaches that this is possible only for a *tzadik*, a consummately holy individual.

In the safety of the counseling context, however, we can "rehearse" the transformation process, so that when we are later confronted with the stimulus that led to dark thoughts, it will no longer have this power over us; we will be able to overcome and transform its negative influence over us into good.

R. suffers from acrophobia. Heights make him dizzy. He loses his sense of balance and is afraid of falling.

He should be taught that his fear of heights is God's way of reminding him to fear Him, the ultimate and absolute height of all reality. He can bolster his fear of God by meditating on God's omnipresence. His enhanced awareness of God's presence in his life—in addition to augmenting his fear of God—will also make him aware of God's providence over him; this will make him feel anchored and stable.

Once he realizes that he should fear only God, his fear of heights becomes sweetened, that is, abstracted to its source. In therapy, his counselor may suggest that he picture himself atop a tall skyscraper experiencing only the fear of God rather than fear of heights. The next time he actually finds himself somewhere high up, he will be more capable of overcoming his phobia.

Just as a newly recruited soldier stands little chance of facing a well-accomplished enemy without going through basic training, we, too, should initially feel too weak to face the power of negativity. We should therefore practice and master the art of war; only then, with God's help, will we win the battle against darkness. Even the boldest and most heroic fighters of the Jewish people, the Maccabees, are called "the weak facing the strong" in our prayers.

We took note above of the relation between evil and fear. We saw how the messianic call to face evil and transform it into good requires, firstly and foremost, the ability to overcome our negative fears or phobias. Through psychological and behavioral re-programming we can meditatively elevate what is evil and transform it into good, but we can only do this after we first become sensitive to the darkness within us.

In our description of the context of positive reinterpretation, we have depicted three stages, which reflect the three stages of psychotherapy as taught by the Ba'al Shem Tov, as follows:

3. sweetening	performing the process in the field
2. separating	rehearsing the process
1. submission	realizing that rehearsal is necessary

TURNING FROM EVIL AND DOING GOOD

The Torah's fundamental attitude toward good and evil is summarized in the verse: "Depart from evil and do good."[15] This disarmingly self-evident statement contains within it radically different understandings of how we may rid ourselves of our inner evil. These different understandings apply at successive stages of an individual's spiritual growth and have received changing emphasis as history has unfolded.

The simple interpretation of this phrase is that we must "depart from evil" before we can hope to "do good." Self-refinement and our relationship with God must be based on renunciation of all wrongful behavior, speech, and thinking. Only then can we begin to do good. This is because as long as we have not banished the evil from within us, any good we will attempt to do will be clouded by that evil and its effectiveness diminished. By way of analogy, common sense dictates that when we prepare a house for a special occasion, we sweep out the dirt before we bring out the fine tableware and decor.

This understanding of the verse has set the tone for Jewish living throughout history. In earlier times, spiritual advancement was seen as being predicated on rigorously ridding the individual of wrongdoing and its effects.

It is true, of course, that the Torah obligates us to fulfill its active commandments (i.e., to "do good") whether or not we have fully "departed from evil." But the awareness of our shortcomings leaves us feeling somehow unworthy of doing good.

The Ba'al Shem Tov points out that this attitude becomes subdued as we climb the ladder of spiritual growth but is never entirely lost. He explains the verse, "there is no righteous person on earth who does good and does not sin"[16] to mean that *every* act of good is tainted with some element of sin—at the very least, with some unwarranted pride in having done good.[17] Thus, even *while* doing good, we must "depart from evil," that is, we must bear in mind the innate egocentricity of our animal soul; this keeps our ego from becoming inflated over the good we do.

A deeper understanding of "depart from evil and do good" is that *"depart from* evil" means *"ignore* evil,"[18] that is, do not allow evil to get in the way of doing good. Rather, rely on the good to overcome and eradicate the evil. When we simply do a little extra good, we find that "even a little light will dispel a great deal of darkness."[19]

The Ba'al Shem Tov offers a third, even deeper interpretation of this phrase: he reads the words "and do good" as "and make it [i.e., the evil itself] good."[20] The ultimate way to get rid of inner evil is to reveal its inner kernel of good, its innate spark of Divinity, which, when revealed, provides us with the power to transform the evil itself into good.[21] As we have seen, this is the culmination of the Kabbalistic therapeutic process.

These three interpretations of "depart from evil and do good" align with the three stages of the Ba'al Shem Tov's model for spiritual growth as follows:

3. sweetening	*depart from evil* by *making* it *good*
2. separation	*depart from evil* by ignoring it and *doing* additional *good*
1. submission	*depart from evil* before *doing good*

Even in the sweetening stage, the objective of turning the evil into good is accomplished by *doing* good. Once we have mentally isolated the kernel of good within the evil, we must actualize it by altering our behavior patterns to manifest this inner good and thereby gain the power to transform the evil itself into good.[22]

UNMASKING THE ILLUSION

The power darkness possesses over us is the power of illusion. Intelligent people do not intentionally harm themselves. Only when they imagine that a particular negative action will not really harm them, or it will do so only temporarily, or the advantages it brings will outweigh the damage, do they engage in wrongdoing.

In the majority of cases, evil succeeds because we delude ourselves into thinking that it is in our *best* interest to succumb to its temptations. The pleasure that often accompanies wrongdoing presents a false promise of a sublime uplifting that, we become convinced, will improve our lives immeasurably. But afterwards, reality hits and we have to admit that, to our chagrin, we were duped. The enticement was a ruse, the lift only momentary, and in its wake we feel shamed and betrayed.

There are two ways to react to such an awakening. We can resolve never to make the same mistake again. The fear of betraying God (and the Godliness within ourselves) motivates us to identify and resist similar illusions. Now that we have risen to a level of consciousness at which it is clear that our previous failings were the result of being fooled, we have retroactively transformed those previous *intentional* transgressions into *unintentional* ones.[23] The only reason we transgressed then is because we were operating under an illusion. Had we known then what we know now, we would never have done what we did.

On a deeper level, we can look back at the transgression we now regret and consider its cause. Was it caused by a promise of some thrill, some rush of exuberance that is sorely missing from our lives? Perhaps we despaired of finding pleasure, exuberance, and self-fulfillment in holy ways. We may have even thought that it is somehow illegitimate or irreverent to seek such experiences in the context of a spiritual life.[24] The logical conclusion of such thinking is that pleasure can be achieved only through transgression.[25]

J. is plagued by wanderlust. He dreams constantly of leaving his wife and family and traveling around the world to explore picturesque and breathtaking sights. These thoughts haunt him constantly, preventing him from concentrating on anything or anyone else and forcing him to spend his last cent on travel magazines and waste hour after hour watching travel programs on television.

If J. were to look at his life a little more closely, he might see that he has straight-jacketed himself into a very mundane existence and left himself little time for relaxation or creative outlets. The first step, then, would be for him to go on a trip once or twice a year.

Beyond that, there lies a legitimate need for a regular dose of the stimulation and excitement that make life interesting and challenging. God wants our lives to be both disciplined *and* inspired, regular *and* spontaneous. J. has focused only on one side and neglected the other.[26] He denies himself the excitement of letting his imagination take him to uncharted realms of his own personality or his relationship with God and the world.

With the best of intentions, J. has stifled an aspect of his personality that is now crying out for attention. If the soul is not given what it needs in a wholesome, holy context, it will produce urges to obtain it in other contexts. By denying himself a constructive outlet for his legitimate urge for stimulation, J. has forced this urge to surface in more destructive ways. The solution here would be for him to allot

himself some time for himself, to follow the trail his Divine soul
wishes to lead him on from time to time.

Alternatively, since God is the ultimate source of all true
life and pleasure,[27] we may have mistaken evil for holiness and
thereby been lured into believing that pursuing a path forbidden by
God will lead us to Him. Here, the promise of God in the
transgression dupes us into committing it. The evil inclination
plays on our innate desire to know God in the fullest way possible.
The *context* of the ploy is indeed evil, but the kernel of it is the
spark of holiness trapped within the forbidden act. Once we
succeed in isolating the holy kernel from the evil context, we may
then focus on it, see what fascination it holds, and reorient it into a
context of holiness. The transgression then serves as the
motivation to seek out God in a more intense way. When we do
this, we have effectively transformed our previous transgressions
into *merits*.[28] Because of the initial wrongdoing, we are now
connecting with God at a higher and more intense level than we
did before.

T. is seeking to improve his spiritual life and level of
religious observance, and is making significant strides. At the
same time, he finds himself spending more and more time
perusing "adult" sites on the Internet. Frustrated and feeling
cheapened each time he does this, he ponders what drives
him to seek such an outlet. He decides to discuss his problem
with a close friend. Together, they conclude that T. is
growing impatient with his spiritual progress and his yearning
for transcendental experience is surfacing as a search for the
quick fix of transitory highs. Aware of the problem, he resolves
both to be more patient and to channel the energy of his
frustration back into his positive spiritual pursuits.

Although it is certainly commendable to resolve never to
make the same mistake again, departing from a wrong path for fear
of where it will lead may leave us paranoid and bitter. Life may

turn into a threatening experience, and we may find ourselves obsessed with fortifying our defenses, building walls to protect ourselves from the world's hostility to Divine consciousness. Every new experience is suspect: is it friend or foe?

In contrast, when we depart from a wrong path by transforming its evil into good, we live in a context of joy, love, and forgiveness. Even though we recognize the evil in the wrong path, we simultaneously recognize its inner reality—misguided good. Without compromising our absolute censure of its evil context, we can focus on the inner core of good within that context. By seeing the good in everything, we empower the good to overcome the evil. This is the deeper reason why the sages instruct us to "judge everyone favorably."[29]

The purpose of Kabbalistic psychotherapy is to enable more and more of the darkness of the subconscious to be illuminated by the light of the conscious. The more the hidden, dark regions of the mind are brought to light, the more they can be elevated into the realm of holiness through the process described above. The more we succeed in exposing and rectifying our darker side, the less will we be plagued by invasive thoughts and urges surfacing from it involuntarily.

This state of freedom from the unrectified, lower self is the true mental well-being sought after by the therapeutic techniques prescribed by Kabbalah and Hassidism. Unhampered by the confines imposed by evil, the creative good in each individual can shine forth and impress its unique expression of Divinity on reality.

In the conflict between light and darkness, light by its very nature wins. If "a little light dispels a lot of darkness," a lot of light will dispel darkness completely and take its place as the rightful inheritor of the mind.

GIVING VOICE TO THE SOUL

As pointed out above,[30] the psychotherapeutic techniques of separation are predicated on the awareness of our inner Divine core, the inner point of pristine goodness within us that cannot be defiled. It is this inner spark, this deepest aspect of our Divine soul, that allows us to engage in positive reinterpretation. Only the part of us that knows only good, that is beyond the reach of evil, can look evil in the face and see only good.

Since this innermost core of our psyche is usually concealed deep within our normal consciousness, coaxing it out of hiding is no simple matter. One of the ways available to us is spontaneous, candid speech.

The Torah identifies the power of speech as the quintessential expression of humanity. Even though our ability to think is far superior to that of the other forms of life, what defines us as uniquely human is our ability to articulate our thoughts and feelings to other human beings.[31] This is because even more than thought, speech has the power to reveal the hidden depths of the soul.

We have all experienced how talking things out, even to ourselves, helps us order and crystallize our thoughts. Often, articulating our thoughts helps us uncover deeper insights and perception into what we are articulating.

The sages teach us that "more understanding was given to woman than to man."[32] One of the mystical interpretations of this saying in Hassidic thought is that man symbolizes silence and woman symbolizes speech.[33] By speaking things out, thereby manifesting our feminine side, we gain additional understanding and reveal hidden depths of our souls. This revelation serves to alleviate—sweeten—our anxiety.

In Hassidic thought, speech is seen as the second of the three means of expression, or "garments," available to the soul, the first being thought and the third being action. An idea born in the mind usually proceeds sequentially through these three "garments": we think about the idea, we talk about it, and finally we act upon it. We generally use speech as a way to express the ideas we have already worked out in our conscious minds.

It would therefore seem that speech can disclose no more to another person than our inner world of thought. The world of conscious thought, however, is quite limited relative to the vast realm of unconscious thought that constitutes the unconscious mind. Speech would thus appear to be restricted to expressing the limited ideas of the conscious mind.

The truth is, however, that speech is not just the end-product of thought; it is an independent "garment" that functions on its own. Just as, at times, we do not talk about our ideas but simply think about them and then act upon them, bypassing speech, so may we at times bypass conscious thought and express in speech an idea originating in the unconscious levels of the mind. This type of speech is spontaneous and unrehearsed, unlike the deliberate speech that expresses the ideas carefully edited and censored by the mind through the faculty of conscious thought. In spontaneous speech, the ideas expressed are the deep, subconscious thoughts that have not been processed or refined by the mind.

As we all know, and as has been observed in conventional psychology, such spontaneous expressions of the subconscious can and do occasionally slip through the censoring process of consciousness and surface unintentionally in the course of conversation, often to our chagrin.[34]

Thus, we see that relaxed, spontaneous speech can reveal both aspects of our soul that are normally obscured by the conscious mind: the inner point of Divine purity and the deep recesses of the unrectified, animal subconscious. This, of course, is as it should be, since we must reveal the former in order to rectify the latter.[35]

If the faculty of speech is to express these dimensions of the mind in a sustained fashion, we must somehow be coaxed into letting our guard down. This can rarely be accomplished directly, with our conscious consent; it is usually the job of our counselor to make us feel comfortable and trusting enough to lull the sentry of our conscious mind into a temporarily dormant state. As we shed the psychological armor we normally wear in order to protect our self-image, we shift into a more natural, spontaneous mode.

However, in coaxing the subconscious to "speak," special care must be exercised in making it reveal its secrets. Otherwise, the effects of doing so can be detrimental rather than beneficial. It is the counselor's role to guide this process, which he does through his choice of words and questions as well as through inexplicit, suggestive nuances of thought, word, and gesture.

It must also be remembered that speech—that is, articulating anxiety—is the final stage of therapy and that we have traveled a long way by this point. The revelations of our unconscious mind will be of a more refined nature than they would have been at the beginning stages of the therapy. Hopefully, they will reveal our innermost point of Divine goodness. At this point, we are anchored in good; this is an essential step in the process of confronting evil, as we shall now see.

THE CONTINUUM OF MORALITY

Kabbalah conceives of good and evil as opposite poles on the continuum of morality. This means that any situation or entity in life contains elements of both good and evil. Our ability to safely descend down the moral continuum toward the pole of evil in order to transform it into good depends on how strongly we are connected to the upper regions of the continuum, near the pole of good. When we are firmly anchored in good—that is, we feel a close relationship with God—we are not afraid to uncover our own dark side nor any evil in the world around us, as its discovery does not pose a threat to our overall belief in the eventual triumph of goodness and holiness.

An essential part of feeling close to God is feeling close to the community of those who have chosen Him as the focus of their lives. Our familial relationship with such a community anchors us in good, enabling us to face evil securely. Moreover, our identification with the community pits the collective goodness of the community against our private evil. This is one reason why Kabbalah and Hassidism have given great weight to brotherly love and communal life alongside personal spiritual growth.

The animal soul, the baser aspect of human nature, pulls us relentlessly toward the pole of evil, away from consciousness of God, while our Divine soul pulls us toward the pole of good. In the words of King Solomon: "...the spirit of man ascends upward, but the spirit of the animal descends below...."[36] Our ability to stay anchored in goodness thus depends on our success in giving our Divine nature precedence over our animal nature.

In the Talmud, we are told of four sages who "entered the orchard"—that is, engaged in mystical meditative techniques and ascended into transcendent realms of Divine consciousness—in order to separate good from evil and thus rectify the moral continuum.

> Ben Azzai gazed [upon the Divine glory] and died; of him Scripture [prophetically] states: "Dear in the estimation of God is the death of His pious ones."[37] Ben Zoma gazed and lost his mind; of him Scripture states: "You have found honey; eat [no more than] your fill, lest you become full and vomit it out."[38] The other one [Elisha ben Avuyah, gazed and] became a heretic. Rabbi Akiva entered in peace and left in peace.[39]

It is explained in Kabbalah[40] that each of these sages attempted to rectify the sin of Adam and its effect on the world. Before the primordial sin, good and evil existed in two separate realms. When Adam and Eve ate the fruit of the tree of knowledge of good and evil, good and evil became intermixed, and the moral continuum was created.

Ben Azzai and Ben Zoma approached the problem from the vantage point of abstract intellect. The problem with this is that good and evil are now so thoroughly intertwined that the force of intellect alone cannot separate them. Ben Azzai sought the transcendent Divine insight that gave rise to creation. In his desire to right the wrong of reality he delved so deep into this mystery that he lost his connection with the world altogether and died. Ben Zoma attempted to understand the inner workings of creation. The experience of this knowledge, abstracted from the issues of life, drove him insane.

Elisha ben Avuyah's mistake was that he tried to rectify the sin by dealing directly with evil and neglected to first anchor himself in good. Focusing entirely on the evil in the world, he lost the ability to reconcile its existence with a benevolent, caring God. The questions posed by evil were too great for him; he came to deny Divine providence and became a heretic.[41]

In contrast, Rabbi Akiva sought to rectify the sin of Adam by emphasizing the good and overcoming evil indirectly. Although he did not succeed in bringing about the Redemption, he nonetheless was able to emerge unscathed from the attempt. Since he remained fixed in the consciousness of God's goodness, the evil in the world did not constitute a contradiction for him.[42]

He maintained this perspective until the end of his life. When caught teaching Torah during the persecutions of the Roman emperor Hadrian, he was sentenced to a terrible death. While the Romans were raking his flesh with iron combs, he recited the *Shema*, the declaration of the unity of God. The existence of evil did not challenge his faith. Rather, his faith and love[43] for God were so strong that he was able to feel close to God even while being tortured to death.

LEAVES OF HEALING

The transformation of the core of evil into good is alluded to allegorically in the Book of Ezekiel. In his depiction of the Temple that will be rebuilt as the center of Jerusalem in the messianic era, Ezekiel describes a wondrous spring whose waters will flow out of the Temple's inner chamber. These waters will become a mighty river that will sweeten the salt water in the oceans (that is, make it drinkable). Trees will grow on the banks of this river, and each tree's "fruit will be for food and its leaves for healing."[44]

Implicit in the Hebrew word used here for "healing" *(terufah)* is the idea of rest and relaxation, which provide release from the tensions and pressures that accompany fears and anxieties.[45] When we are relieved of stress, proper flow is restored to both the physiological and psychological systems of the body; thus, relaxation is essential to mental and physical health. Part of this relaxation process is, of course, the opportunity to express and release our worries and fears freely, which ultimately leads to psychological healing.[46]

In the imagery of Ezekiel's prophecy, the source of this healing relaxation is the leaf. Compared to the tree itself or its fruit, a leaf appears to be secondary, a minor detail often unappreciated, even though it performs the crucial function of photosynthesis. Similarly, we generally ignore our unconscious mind and pay little heed to the crucial ways in which it affects our lives. However, as we have seen, hidden Divine light is transformed into new life-force in the unconscious realms of the soul, a process of spiritual photosynthesis.[47] The leaf is thus an apt metaphor for the unconscious.

The leaf, the unconscious, holds the key to the ultimate healing of the psyche. Today, through photosynthesis, the leaf produces food (carbohydrates); in the future, the leaf itself will become edible, like fruit. This means that with the complete transformation of evil into good, the unconscious will be able to be fully expressed, because all the strictures surrounding its articulation will be relaxed.

The beginning of the Book of Psalms makes use of similar imagery:

> Happy is the person who has not followed the
> advice of the evil ones…but rather desires [only]
> God's Torah…. He shall be like a tree planted
> beside streams of water, which yields its fruit in
> the proper season, whose leaves never wilt, and
> whatever he does will prosper.[48]

Here, a good person is likened to a tree planted beside life-giving water. The leaf that does not wilt is his unconscious, which he has sweetened through articulation. He has accomplished this after going through the phases of submission (not following the advice of the "evil ones") and separation (desiring and learning God's Torah).

As noted earlier, the Ba'al Shem Tov recognized God's providence over all His creatures by observing the way a leaf fell from a tree and was blown along the ground. By taking note of a seemingly insignificant factor in the great scheme of creation, the Ba'al Shem Tov discerned the truth that was to serve as the cornerstone of his theological system.

The sages interpret the imagery of the leaf in the verse quoted above to refer to the seemingly mundane conversation of Torah scholars.[49] Unlike the chatter of the unlettered, the mundane conversation of someone who is filled with the wisdom of the Torah is itself a lesson in holy living and considered a subject worthy of study (and thus "never wilts"). The lessons of life that surface in the mundane conversation of a Torah scholar reflect the way he has rectified his unconscious mind. When we absorb the attitudes expressed in his words, we absorb something of his positive, constructive outlook on life. As such, his mundane conversation—his "leaf"—can serve as a source of optimism and healing for those who seek his counsel.

8
Kabbalistic vs. Conventional Psychology

We are taught that the Torah is God's "blueprint" for creation, that is, that He created the world according to the way the world is described in the Torah.[1] This means that the Torah implicitly contains the deepest and most precise understanding of all aspects of reality. However, not all of this depth is explicit; uncovering the Torah's truths is an ongoing process that God has given to us to complete. This process occurs in two directions. On the one hand, we continuously mine the Torah's text and oral traditions for deeper and deeper insights. On the other hand, we amass empirical data from the observable world and form theories to explain our findings. In order to arrive at a true picture of reality, we see how our empirical findings compare with our understanding of the Torah, or vice versa.

If we confront an apparent discrepancy, this encourages us to seek an explanation. Perhaps our data is incomplete and we have to test the field more thoroughly. Or perhaps we have to find a deeper level of understanding in the Torah that will encompass our empirical findings. In this way, Torah study and human inquiry benefit from mutual cross-fertilization: the empirical findings and the theories they spawn serve to direct our exploration of the Torah and help us uncover new insights that will encompass them, while the absolute precision of the Torah's worldview directs our interpretation of our empirical findings.

In any event, the more refined our understanding of any particular discipline or aspect of reality, the more we may expect it to mirror the Torah's view of this same discipline. Nonetheless, as long as the secular discipline does not take into account the existence, presence, and influence of God, this resemblance remains merely superficial.

Modern methods of conventional psychotherapy do, in fact, resemble the Torah-based process of submission, separation, and sweetening we have been describing.

Conventional psychology's submission phase consists of its extensive preoccupation with "limits" and "boundaries." In the course of therapy, the patient is required to give due attention to the "contract" between himself and the therapist, which outlines what is appropriate and inappropriate behavior inside and outside the therapist's office. Accepting these limitations involves a form of submission, but there is still considerable difference in essence between acceding to rules and truly humbling the ego in recognition of the greatness and goodness of God.

The separation stage comes to play in conventional psychotherapy in the dialogue between the therapist and the patient when the distinction is drawn between those aspects of the patient's psyche which are intrinsic to him and those which originate outside of him. Very often, in the course of such a discussion, the patient comes to realize that the negative elements which he has considered part and parcel of his personality are, in fact, external baggage which has been grafted onto him and which he need not continue to carry. Here the distinction (separation) is made between the patient's true inner self and the outer, nonessential crust that encompasses him.

Nonetheless, as conventional psychology does not recognize the existence of the Divine soul, it is unable to see any redeeming value in the process of separation prescribed by the Kabbalah—that is, ignoring problems or the past traumas that gave rise to them. For the conventional psychologist, this is "repression," the psyche's refusal to face its true self and allow the thoughts and impulses buried in the darkness of its subconscious to surface.

Of course, Kabbalistic psychotherapy also considers repression a negative psychological phenomenon, for it denies the existence of a problem or past trauma and pretends it does not exist. When thoughts, impulses, and urges are repressed, they will only fester within the subconscious, eventually to resurface in a much more detrimental form. The submission and separation we have been discussing here are not repressive. Rather, they are conscious efforts to neutralize our exaggerated ego and exaggerated obsessions with our problems (submission), followed by efforts to pursue and focus on good by ignoring evil (separation). Neither of these forms of suppression implies denial of our problems or their causes.

The conventional psychotherapist, who attributes no intrinsic value to ignoring a problem, will tend to encourage his patients to deal with their psychological problems as soon as possible. He reasons that just as it is best to deal with medical problems as soon as they arise and not ignore them, it is best to deal with psychological problems as soon as they surface. The second stage of the Kabbalistic system, ignoring anxiety in order to allow the Divine soul to manifest itself, cannot, therefore, be a part of conventional psychotherapy.

The sweetening phase of conventional psychological therapy is described graphically in the more recent psychological theories, according to which the therapist often plays the role of a mother reflecting back her child's good points. As the good expands in the patient's consciousness, the ailing psyche of the patient is theoretically healed. But, as noted above,[2] a frank assessment of an unrectified life will typically reveal that the good points of our personalities are far outweighed by the bad points. This technique is therefore a far cry from true sweetening, an experience of God's infinite light penetrating and permeating all of one's being.

Moreover, conventional psychology warns against mistiming (what we might call premature sweetening) on the part of the therapist, who is advised not to raise difficult problems before the time is ripe for dealing with them. Bad timing is likely to lead to a negative reaction from the patient and may not only impair the therapeutic process but possibly damage the patient. Here, the necessity to wait until the time is ripe (to predicate sweetening on separation) is merely *de facto*, and is not based on the recognition of the intrinsic value inherent in the separation process, as described above.

All the above serves to illustrate the fact that although there appear to be external resemblances between conventional psychology and the process described here, there remains an essential difference: conventional psychology is limited by the boundaries of the patient's animal soul and the human intellect of the therapist, while the Kabbalistic therapeutic practices derive their effectiveness from the revelation of the infinite powers of the Divine soul and its connection to its Divine source.

THE ERROR OF BYPASSING SEPARATION

Clearly, then, of all three stages, submission, separation, and sweetening, the stage in which the conventional version is most explicitly unlike its Kabbalistic counterpart is the stage of separation. Conventional psychology, which is based on human intellect rather than on the Divine wisdom of the Torah and its absolute definitions of right and wrong, cannot grasp the real dividing line between good and evil. This is why conventional psychotherapy sees no value in ignoring anxiety—in its eyes, there is no absolute good to be revealed by doing so.

This is a classic example of the common human failing of seeking to skip directly from submission to sweetening without undergoing the intermediate, prerequisite stage of separation. This mistake is common not only in the conventional context but also among Torah-oriented individuals.[3]

The temptation to do this arises from the fact that there is indeed a type of sweetening in the submission stage itself (not to be confused with the sub-phase we have identified above as sweetening within submission), albeit in a subdued form. The force of ego is so pervasive in the human psyche that as soon as we begin to wean ourselves of our self-centeredness, we are consciously or subconsciously struck by our oneness with every element of creation. This perception sweetens reality and changes the individual's attitude toward the rest of creation from one of exploitation to one of concern, respect, or perhaps even love.

The inherent problem here is that this revelation may result in an anarchy of values that can eventually lead to absurd and even destructive conclusions. It is all well and good to aspire to be "at one" with creation, but do we really want to be "at one" with starvation, war, disease, oppression, cruelty, brute force, terrorism, substance abuse, pornography, emptiness, and boredom? Without a clear-cut means of drawing boundaries, these aspects of life can claim legitimacy along with the rest. Separation of good and evil is therefore necessary to make this nascent sweetening real. Throughout history, this has been the fundamental and fatal error in all attempts to rectify reality, impel society toward utopia, or hasten the advent of the Messiah.[4]

Only after having established the boundaries between good and evil and having become practiced in the art of ignoring evil is it possible to proceed to the next stage, sweetening. Only then can we begin to examine, identify, and expose the hidden recesses of the subconscious mind in order to transform this dark, unholy realm into light. As we have noted, this is the mystical significance of how God created light and darkness: "And God called the light day and the darkness He called night"—that is, He gave each its own defined domain—"and there was evening and there was morning, one day"[5]—that is, only then could all be sweetened and become part of the unity of creation.

PERMISSIVENESS AND SWEETENING

Since conventional psychology does not possess any absolute criteria for determining what is permitted or forbidden, it must adopt the attitude of "innocent until proven guilty": there is nothing inherently wrong with any particular type of behavior until it can be empirically demonstrated that it is detrimental, either to the individual or to society. (Even then, the secular outlook would be hard-pressed to brand a censored behavior *intrinsically* or *essentially* wrong. The most the honest secularist can say is that, given the psychosocial context in which we live, a certain behavior has harmful consequences.) Conventional psychology therefore inherently tends toward permissiveness, the attitude that everything is essentially legitimate.[6]

According to this secular outlook, the best way to solve any psychological problem is to be as uninhibited and unrestrained about it as possible, allowing the individual's natural desires as much free reign as possible to seek out their fulfillment. Even when it is clear that these drives need to be sublimated, many streams in conventional psychotherapy will still look for ways permitted by society to fulfill them. From this secular viewpoint, the absolute value-system of the Torah is virtually meaningless.[7]

In contrast, the "permissiveness" mandated in the sweetening phase of Kabbalistic therapy, which is carried out only after the preliminary phases of submission and separation, does not constitute a release from any of the prohibitions legislated in the Torah.

(There are extremely rare cases in which the Torah itself enjoins the individual to temporarily perform a normally forbidden act or refrain from performing a normally mandated act, for the sake of God.[8] The parameters that define when and how they apply are outside the scope of the present discussion.[9])

The well-known saying of the sages—"one should always use his left hand to push away and his right hand to draw near"[10]—can be applied to the relationship between separation and sweetening. In separation, we use our spiritual "left hand to push away," while in sweetening, we use our spiritual "right hand to draw near."

This reversal occurs as follows: While we are going through the separation phase of our spiritual makeover, we must remain aware that indulging in physical pleasures can be detrimental to our spiritual growth. True, the Torah allows a person to indulge in worldly pleasures as long as doing so involves no overt transgression of any of its prohibitions. At this stage, however, we are not spiritually advanced enough to allow ourselves this luxury. Although we are cautioned to avoid asceticism, we are also commanded to follow the sages' advice: "Sanctify yourself [even] with regard to that which is [otherwise] permitted to you."[11] We must strive to abstain from the sensual pleasures this world offers unless they form an essential part of our Divine service, such as when we enjoy fine food and drink in honor of Shabbat or in order to open our hearts to the study of the Torah and the performance of its commandments in joy.[12]

In contrast, when we reach the stage of sweetening and have extricated ourselves from the self-orientation of the unrectified ego, we may indeed begin to savor all the delights God has placed in the world for our enjoyment. In this context, the advice of the sages to "sanctify yourself with regard to that which is permitted to you" means, "infuse your holy attitude toward life in all the pleasures permitted you." At this level, all our deeds are truly and intrinsically "for the sake of heaven." This is how Hassidic thought interprets King Solomon's directive, "Know Him in all your ways"[13] and the sages' assertion that we will eventually be called to account for all the pleasures that we could have enjoyed in this world but abstained from.[14]

This Torah-sanctioned sweetening of life gives God great pleasure, so to speak, because, after all, He created this world as a vehicle for giving pleasure to His creatures.[15] Still, we cannot enjoy the world in the way that God intended us to unless we have reached the level of constant awareness of His presence in our lives.

We can be constantly aware of God even as we enjoy the pleasures of His world only insofar as we have accomplished the goals of separation. Once we have experienced the true delight of being close to God, the superficial enticements of this world no longer impress us, and we no longer feel compelled to exert ourselves to obtain them and indulge in them.

At this stage, when we do indulge in some physical enjoyment, we do so in an essentially liberated way: we experience the pleasure as pure and unadulterated instead of the fulfillment of some artificial need. More importantly, since we are in no way captives of the pleasure in which we indulge, we can freely experience it as part of our overall connection to God.

9
The Therapist at Work

As we noted earlier,[1] the role of the counselor or therapist can be filled by one's spouse, a close friend, or a spiritual mentor or advisor. Whoever fulfills this role can best do so if he or she has conscientiously and earnestly endeavored to study, internalize, and fulfill the teachings of Kabbalah and Hassidism in his daily life. By persistently refining his own character, and especially by practicing and acquiring humility through ongoing self-examination, a person acquires the ability to understand and assist those who seek his counsel. (This is somewhat similar to the requirement in conventional psychoanalysis that every psychoanalyst himself undergo psychoanalysis.)

At first glance, it would seem that a truly humble person would shun the role of guiding the spiritual growth of others. After all, isn't it presumptuous for us to assume that we have internalized the necessary teachings enough to be able to guide someone else who has not progressed as far along the way? Shouldn't the spiritually-oriented person be wary of the inevitable feeling of self-satisfaction that come with successfully solving other people's problems?

To the contrary: the truly humble person will humble himself before the truth. He will be as aware of his own experience, gifts, and talents as he will be of his shortcomings and the long road still ahead. Moreover, he will give no thought to his own interests and the spiritual risks that helping others entails. When called upon, he will assume the role of counselor with grace and conviction and not evade his responsibility for reasons of false modesty. As Rabbi Menachem Mendel Schneersohn, the Lubavitcher *Rebbe*, put it, if all a person knows is the first letter of the alphabet and there is another who does not know even that, the one who knows a little is obligated to teach the one who knows nothing before he himself goes on to learn more.[2]

In any case, the assured resolution of the problem can never be ascribed solely to the sensitivity and good advice of the counselor or therapist, because the person seeking help plays an active role in the discussion of the problem and the effort to solve it. In effect, then, the Divine souls of both join together in the struggle. The odds are thus weighted in favor of good, and evil effectively has no chance.[3]

Hassidism is so confident of the human ability to overcome evil and ultimately transform it into good (providing the requisite conditions have been met) and attaches such great importance to this endeavor that it considers it the central challenge of any true educator, and by extension, any counselor, therapist, or mentor. Since we are laden from birth with predominantly animalistic drives and tendencies,[4] weeding them out is considered the first goal the sincere and dedicated educator should set for himself *vis-à-vis* his charges. His responsibility in this regard is grave indeed: if he does not succeed in rectifying his pupils' negative character traits, he will only make matters worse by having exposed these traits.[5]

The Biblical role model every Hassidic educator, counselor, or therapist should set for himself is, again, Joseph. As the archetypal dreamer and dream interpreter of the Torah, Joseph embodies the ability to reorder the chaotic meanderings of the unrectified imagination[6] or subconscious into meaningful messages that serve as keys to the hidden recesses of the heart and mind.

Joseph was able to do this more than any other Biblical figure because he had successfully wrestled with sexual temptation. In Egypt, a land infamous for its licentiousness and sexual depravity, it would have been the simplest and most natural thing for him to indulge in any of a plethora of sexual enticements. Yet, the Torah relates that he resisted the overtures of his master's wife. For this reason, Jewish tradition calls him "Joseph *the righteous.*"

Modern psychology has correctly verified that many, if not most, neuroses and even psychoses are connected with and derive from sexual perversion, which itself is the consequence of an unrectified ego. According to Kabbalah, each of us is half of a soul that is separated at conception into its male and female components. We are all, therefore, born with a natural urge to find our lost soul-mate. This urge lies at the bottom of our sense of sexuality. Ideally, we should channel the power of this urge into finding our lost soul-mate, on whom we then focus our sexuality exclusively. However, in our subconscious impatience to reunite with our other half, we may succumb to delusions that entice us with the promise of sexual fulfillment. But since these illusions are not our real soul-mate, they will only frustrate us and derail our sexual energy. Such subconscious confusion often undermines our psychological well-being throughout life. Conversely, by staying true to our quest for our true soul-mate, we can largely preserve our psychological clarity.

Thus, it was because of the uncompromised purity of his sexuality that Joseph was able to so successfully help others sort out their complex psychological problems.

Previously, we identified the Joseph within as our ability to replace negative thoughts with positive ones, an aspect of the second phase of therapy, ignoring anxiety. Here, we are identifying him with his more prominent role in the Torah, that of the skilled confidant—the third phase of therapy, articulating anxiety.

As such, Joseph is the archetypal spiritual advisor. Throughout Jewish history, all true shepherds of the flock of Israel and all sincere counselors, mentors, educators, confidants, and therapists have drawn their inspiration from him.

SUBMISSION, SEPARATION, AND SWEETENING IN THE THERAPIST

Until now, we have described the submission, separation, and sweetening process a person must undergo when he or she suffers from psychological problems. The counselor must also undergo his or her own version of the same threefold process in order to truly empathize with the person seeking his or her counsel. We shall now describe this process.

The counselor must be focused, silencing the voices within his mind competing for his attention. This corresponds to the meaning of the first syllable of the word *chashmal*—"silence."

Focusing so completely is only possible when the counselor is motivated by true love, based on the fundamental encounter between his soul and that of the person seeking his counsel. This love is what makes the difference between shallow interest (or worse, mercenary motivations) and true concern. It is possible only when the counselor bears no attitude of condescension toward the sufferer and considers it wholly unnatural and even uncomfortable that he is acting as the therapist and the person before him is acting as the patient. Rather, he should feel that it is just Divine providence that it happened this way, and the roles could just as easily have been reversed—and they may well be in the future. As King Solomon teaches:

> I returned and saw under the sun that the race is not won by the swift, nor the battle by the strong, nor is bread won by the wise, nor wealth by men of understanding, nor favor by men of skill; but time and chance happens to them all.[7]

And as the sages also teach:

> There is a wheel of fortune that spins in the world; he who is rich today may not be rich tomorrow, and he who is poor today may not be poor tomorrow.[8]

These words are as true of mental well-being and all the things that promote tranquility of the mind as they are of physical wealth. This feeling of commonality with the person before him that the counselor must cultivate is his submission.

His separation is the inner filtering process he must undergo while he listens to the person confiding in him. He must sift through the different responses that occur to him, first weeding out those responses that originate in the yet-unrectified regions of his own psyche, and then weeding out those responses that do originate in a good place but are more relevant to himself than to the person before him. Once this is done, he must file away the rejected responses for his own later reflection in order to ensure that they do not color his attitude during counseling.

The counselor's sweetening stage begins when he chooses to view these unwanted and irrelevant responses from a deeper perspective and realizes that they are a blessing in disguise. Divine providence has sent the suffering person to him in order to indirectly make him aware of those areas of his own psyche that require further treatment.

The sages say, "Who is wise? He who learns from everyone."[9] According to the Ba'al Shem Tov, this includes even learning from the behavior or attitude of an evil person. We must learn to find the same faults in ourselves that we perceive in others—even if in a more abstract or refined way. Since we generally do not notice our own faults, God often makes us aware of them by mirroring them to us in other people. Only when we rectify the fault in ourselves, the Ba'al Shem Tov concludes, are we able to help the person in whom we observed the fault, as well.[10]

We can also learn positive lessons from the negative behavior we observe in others, since character traits that are evil in one context may be good in another.

Rabbi Zushya of Anipol learned seven ways to serve God from the behavior of thieves: discretion, daring, attention to detail, industriousness, alacrity, optimism, and persistence.[11]***

Not only must the therapist find the problems of the person seeking his counsel in himself, he must fully empathize with him. He must move cautiously between full subjective identification with the world of the person seeking his counsel and the objective distance which affords him a clear perspective.[12]

> During the course of receiving individuals for private counseling, Rabbi Dovber of Lubavitch[13] would become soaking wet from perspiration. When asked why, he explained that when someone enters his study and asks for advice, he must metaphorically divest himself of his own "clothes" and put on the "clothes" of that person in order to fully identify with him. Then, he has to re-don his own "clothes" in order to view the problem objectively and offer advice from his own perspective. The effort expended in doing this repeatedly caused him to sweat so profusely.

His own process of submission, separation, and sweetening renders the therapist increasingly sensitive to the person seeking his counsel, and, at the same time, allows him to maintain proper balance between subjectivity and objectivity. He learns to "listen with the third ear"; deep, inner silence pervades his stages of silence, severing, and speech. Although both the counselor and the counseled must pass through the three stages of silence, severing, and speech (the paradox of *chashmal*), the counselor must strive to be relatively silent, allowing the person seeking his counsel to speak.[14]

To summarize:

3. sweetening	speech	learning from the person seeking help
2. separation	severing	inner filtering, sifting through possible responses
1. submission	silence	focusing of attention, silencing of other voices

Moreover, if we closely examine the psychological workings within the therapist himself as outlined above, we can discern the full, ninefold inter-inclusion of submission, separation, and sweetening:[15]

3. sweetening	sweetening	helping the other person rectify his problem
	separation	rectifying the fault in himself
	submission	seeing the other person's faults in himself
2. separation	sweetening	finding the right words to say to the other person
	separation	differentiating between responses relevant to himself and those relevant to the other person
	submission	recognizing responses arising from the unrectified regions of his own psyche
1. submission	sweetening	focusing on the other person with love, based on commonality
	separation	assuming the role of the therapist nonetheless
	submission	feeling of commonality with the person seeking counsel

THE VALUE OF ONGOING THERAPY

We noted at the outset[16] that is highly commendable for every person pursuing a path of spiritual growth to maintain an ongoing relationship with a counselor, advisor, or therapist. As the Talmud advises: "Appoint yourself a mentor."[17] We should feel comfortable in discussing any of our problems, anxieties, and insecurities, especially those which concern our relationship with God, with this individual.[18]

Furthermore, it is helpful to regularly discuss our inner world of thought and emotion with our counselor, even if we are not suffering from any particular anxiety or problem. When we articulate our inner thoughts and share them with someone else, we tend to explore them more deeply and more seriously than we might otherwise. We must face our inner thoughts and integrate them into the whole picture of ourselves if our discussions with our counselor are to be productive and real.

G. had a bad day at work. Instead of going home anxious or depressed, he first shares his feelings with his mentor. G.'s mentor reminds him about Divine providence and helps him humble his ego. The discussion also helps him concentrate his thoughts and efforts on the well-being of others, not just on himself.

When he goes home, his peaceful disposition, despite his troubles, enables him to appreciate the material and spiritual blessings God has blessed him with, and will enable him to receive even more. As the sages teach: "The Holy One, blessed be He, found no vessel as worthy to contain blessing for Israel as peace, as it is written, 'God will give His people strength; God will bless His people with peace.'"[19]

In addition, an essential institution of Hassidic lifestyle is its equivalent of "group therapy," the Hassidic *farbrengen* ("get-together"). In a *farbrengen*, against a backdrop of song, stories, and words of Torah, Hassidim bless one another with *l'chaim* and pour out their hearts to one another as they reveal their deepest feelings and seek counsel from the elders of the community and their closest friends.

10
Positive Anxiety

ANXIETY AS INSPIRATION

It is clear that when left untreated, anxiety will certainly have negative effects on our mental well-being. However, when treated properly, anxiety and its causes can actually be a boon to our mental and spiritual development. Anxiety is not something negative *per se*; only when left to fester untreated does it manifest itself in negative ways.

In addition, there is a form of anxiety that directly and positively contributes to our overall well-being and motivates us toward inspired and even altruistic action. Here, anxiety is caring—feeling deep concern for all of God's creations—the antithesis of apathy.

Referring to this positive anxiety, the sages assert that God reveals His secrets only to an anxious person: "The mysteries of the Torah are only revealed to one whose heart is anxious within him."[1] In other words, there is a type of anxiety that is a *requirement* for understanding the inner dimension of the Torah. There is evidently some redeeming value in this type of anxiety that makes those who suffer from it capable of understanding and relating to the hidden meaning of God's word.

111

The Torah is an extensive body of knowledge, both with regard to the amount of information it encompasses and the types of knowledge it comprises. The most basic type of knowledge the Torah contains is how we should conduct our lives in order to fulfill God's will; this is why it is called "a Torah of life."[2] This body of knowledge is the legal aspect of the Torah, and includes the commandments, their derivations, and the methodology for formulating new rules for new circumstances. Inasmuch as the same laws of conduct apply to everyone, this body of knowledge is called the "revealed" aspect of the Torah. The duty to know and understand the law applies equally to all; we all must know how to conduct our lives in accordance with God's will, so we all must study the revealed aspect of the Torah.

Success in the study of this aspect of the Torah does not depend on any moral achievements or special qualities. It depends solely on the quality and quantity of the sincere effort we expend in its pursuit. Whoever applies himself or herself properly to this goal is assured of realizing it.[3]

The inner strata of the Torah, however, do not deal with common standards of behavior but with our inner cognitive and emotional life and the dynamics of our personal relationship with God. Since everyone's personality is different, this aspect of the Torah is much more subjective than the revealed aspect. It is therefore known as the "hidden" aspect of the Torah, since it addresses the personal issues of our lives, which are generally hidden from other people.[4]

Effort and dedication are not enough to ensure success in the study of this aspect of the Torah; here, the experience of anxiety is required as well.

This is because the secrets of the Torah shed light on the existential problems of humanity and the world at large. They are a comprehensive answer to the world's most essential and pivotal problems. But if there is no question, there is no need for an answer. Thus, only those who are bothered by the incongruities of life, whose souls cry out for a solution to all the seemingly unsolvable questions life presents, can hope to relate to this aspect of the Torah. Those who are not bothered by questions such as "Why was I created?" or "Why is there evil and suffering in the world?" will neither be drawn to the study of the inner dimension of the Torah, nor will it speak to them.

Suffering from some form of anxiety betrays a certain sensitivity, feeling, and caring. Those who do not suffer from anxiety have no sense of pathos in their lives. They are thus indifferent to the questions addressed by the secrets of the Torah.[5]

AWAITING THE MESSIAH

All our personal problems are reflections of the more universal problem that life in general is not the way it ought to be. Consciously or unconsciously, we realize that the world is not perfect and that its imperfection is not just the result of a few minor flaws. Rather, there is something fundamentally wrong, inconsistent, and abnormal about the very fiber of existence.

The Torah in fact tells us that the world is not presently in the state God intended for it, and promises us that one day He will redeem it from its fallen status and restore it to its original healthy, fully-functioning condition. In the words of the prophet Isaiah:

> In the days to come, the Mount of God's House
> shall stand firm above the mountains and tower

above the hills. And all the nations shall stream
to it. And the many peoples shall go and say:
"Come, let us go up to the Mount of God, to
the House of the God of Jacob—that He may
instruct us in His ways, that we may walk in His
paths." For from Zion shall come forth the
Torah, and the word of God from Jerusalem.[6]

The Redemption is thus the answer to all of life's travails,
for all natural and psychological problems are born of the fallen
consciousness that will be healed when it arrives. Therefore, the
essential existential questions of life can all be telescoped into one,
general question: Why has the Redemption not yet occurred?

The Torah's scenario of redemption centers on the figure
of the Messiah. The Messiah (Hebrew: *Mashiach*, meaning
"anointed one") is a human descendant of King David, who will
use his innate qualities of leadership and his knowledge of the
Torah to bring the Jewish people back to Israel, inspire the entire
world to believe in the one God, and usher in an era of universal
peace and brotherhood.

Although belief in the coming of the Messiah is one of the
thirteen basic principles of the Jewish faith,[7] the extent to which
this tenet of faith is intended to forge our consciousness[8] is
unfortunately widely unappreciated, or even unknown. Even
among those who are aware of the centrality of this concept in
Judaism, it is commonly assumed that the advent of the Messiah is
not something we need to be concerned with or actively seek to
hasten.

In fact, however, the Redemption is not only one of the
basic principles of Judaism, but the central focus and underlying
thrust of Jewish life. Our belief in the Redemption expresses our

radical non-acceptance of reality as it is, our bold refusal to be satisfied with the present order.

For the caring person, the Redemption is not an abstract aspiration we aim toward in our struggles with life; it is crucial, a necessity, an ontological imperative. The fact that the Messiah has not yet come and the Redemption seems far off is cause for our gravest, unceasing concern. The puzzle behind the delay in his arrival must be solved.

As we said, all other anxieties can be reduced to this one, ultimate anxiety. Thus, the extent to which we are concerned only with our private anxieties and problems is inversely indicative of how seriously we take them. By not seeing our concerns as part of the common angst of humanity, we are testifying that our problems do not bother us enough to motivate us to do away with the underlying reason for their existence. We would be happy to settle for a temporary bandage, alleviate our immediate pain, and get on with life. By universalizing the scope of our concerns, we are demonstrating our desire to put reality back on track— including our own reality—once and for all.

Rabbi Menachem Mendel Schneersohn, the Lubavitcher *Rebbe*, said that the foremost reason the Redemption has not yet come is that we do not sufficiently yearn for it.[9] By being truly anxious over the Messiah's absence, we hasten his arrival. As the *Rebbe* stated repeatedly, had we truly wanted the Messiah to come he would have come long ago.

Even those who have undergone the full psycho-therapeutic process detailed above and have ascended the ladder of spirituality to the point where their consciousness is wholly that of their Divine soul are not immune to this ultimate anxiety. Even though they have made peace with all their personal anxieties, they are still plagued by the one, basic anxiety that results from the inherent limitations of creation.[10]

In the course of "descending" into the body, the soul loses the infinite perception of Divinity it enjoyed beforehand. Entering the physical world, the soul is forced to relate to everything in the finite context of time and space. It is next to impossible for the mind to imagine a level of reality outside these limitations. Those who are attuned to this fact, and whose hearts' desire is to know and cleave to God, are fundamentally frustrated by this reality.

Thus, even the holiest individuals, the paragons of spiritual perfection, are subject to profound anxiety and suffering by the simple virtue of being human. They are trapped, as we all are, in the limitations and conceptual modes of the physical world that will not disappear until the messianic era.[11] This condition, coupled with their sincere concern with the plight of humanity and reality at large, makes such individuals yearn for the Redemption and be concerned about hastening it more than anyone else.

Despite the profound intensity of messianic anxiety, it is subdued in its nature. As a non-specific reaction to the general state of reality rather than a response to a specific problem, it underlies the whole of life subliminally. Unlike other forms of anxiety that may impair our ability to function normally, this super-anxiety (or sub-anxiety) does not incapacitate us in any way.[12] On the contrary, it inspires us and fills us with the positive energy and joy of optimistic purpose.

This psychological polarity of anxiety vs. cheerfulness is characteristic of the inner dimension of the Torah, which enables us effectively to live in a state of paradox. In the words of the *Zohar*: "Weeping is wedged in my heart on this side, and joy is wedged in my heart on the other."[13]

Whatever form it takes, anxiety over the coming of the Messiah both focuses and intensifies our concern with the incompleteness of life. When we generalize this concern to the overall, unredeemed condition of reality—whether on the level of common human suffering or the existential constrictions of creation—our anxiety takes on a more profound meaning. Thus, if existential anxiety in general prepares us for the study of the inner dimension of the Torah, existential anxiety over the coming of the Messiah prepares us for the ultimate revelation of the inner dimension of the Torah that will accompany the advent of the Messianic era. For the inner dimension of the Torah that we know today is but a foretaste of the revelation we will witness with the Redemption.[14]

THE SPARK OF THE MESSIAH

According to Kabbalah, every Jew has within him a "spark" of the Messiah.[15] This spark is our drive and capacity to act as a redeeming force for ourselves, for those we know, and for everything in the world with which we come in contact.

Just as the arrival of the Messiah depends on and is hastened by our anxiety over his delay, the actualization of the messianic spark within us requires first that we be anxious over the fact that it has not yet manifested itself.

The deepest complex in our psyche is the frustration we feel over not being able to fully actualize our potential, to live up to what we feel we are capable of becoming. Deep down, we know that our soul is a part of God and through it we are capable of revealing God's presence in the world. The fact that we are prevented from doing so troubles us deeply.

This frustration is equivalent to anxiety over not being able to actualize our inner messianic spark; it is the messianic spark within each of us that gives rise to this existential anxiety. The more we think about the purpose of life and the urgency of rectifying reality, the more intense this anxiety becomes. As noted earlier, this anxiety sensitizes us to the inner dimension of the Torah. Although the study of the Torah's inner dimension serves to heighten our awareness of the urgent need for redemption, it also bolsters our belief and optimism that redemption is imminent. This serves to take the edge off the bitterness of our anxiety without mitigating its intensity.

The revelation of the messianic spark does not happen all at once. Inasmuch as the Divine soul embodies infinite layers of potential, as soon as we actualize and exhaust one level of our Divine potential, deeper, more powerful levels become accessible to us and challenge us to reveal our messianic spark at this deeper level of Divine potential.

In other words, progressing on the path of spiritual growth is akin to climbing a spiral staircase. The ongoing dynamic of tension and fulfillment spurs us to realize our messianic spark, our ability to redeem the world, on continuously higher levels. The greater our anxiety, the more we are inspired to deepen our relationship with God, delve into the secrets of the Torah, and reveal our inner spark. In turn, the more we deepen our relationship with God, study the inner dimension of the Torah, and become inspired to redeem the world, the more we feel the urgency of redemption and our anxiety over its delay intensifies. Because the Torah is infinite and every understanding of life it gives us is also infinite, every answer to life's anomalies the Torah offers gives rise to another, deeper question in its wake. Each level of understanding is replaced by a succeeding, deeper level.

This ongoing dynamic of tension and resolution is necessary for our continued spiritual growth. With every answer—with every new, comprehensive understanding of reality—comes a sense of satisfaction at having achieved it. This satisfaction naturally spawns complacency: the problem is solved, we have the answer. And there is nothing that feeds the ego more than the feeling that we possess all the answers. It is therefore necessary to prevent this by asking a new, deeper question immediately upon finding the answer to the previous one.

Of course, the infinity of this process does not mean that it will never reach its conclusion. It is taught in Kabbalah and Hassidism that when a certain critical mass of the individual sparks of the Messiah is actualized, the Messiah himself will be revealed and the ultimate, final Redemption will occur.

SUBMISSION, SEPARATION, AND SWEETENING IN THE MESSIAH

Since the actualization of the spark of the Messiah within each individual is a process of ongoing spiritual growth, it is logical to assume that this process exhibits the same threefold structure that typifies any spiritual growth process.

The feeling of helplessness in the face of a world that is imperfect and incomplete, which translates into anxiety over the delay in the coming of the Messiah, is the submission stage.

The sages teach us that "the Messiah will only come when he is not being thought about."[16] Although this statement seems to imply that the best way to hasten the coming of the Messiah is to ignore the subject, this obviously cannot be the sages' intention, for they clearly declared that constant expectation of the Messianic era is a fundamental tenet of Jewish faith. In the words of the prophet Habakkuk: "If he tarries, wait for him, for he will surely come, without delay."[17]

Rather, "the Messiah will only come when he is not being thought about" means that "the Messiah will come when he is least expected," that is, we should await his imminent arrival even though the world seems unprepared and unworthy of it. The prophets themselves have indicated that the Redemption will come as a complete surprise: "Behold, I am sending My messenger, and he will clear a path before Me; *suddenly* the Master whom you seek will come to His sanctuary...."[18]

There are many signs—both those empirically evident and those foretold by the sages—that the present era is ripe for the Redemption, but in many ways it appears to be far from ready. The situation of the world is such that no one would think the Messiah could come now, yet we believe that reality has reached the critical mass of spirituality necessary for him to arrive, thanks to generations of prayer, Torah study, and self-sacrifice.

This is the separation stage in the process of the revelation of the Messiah, in which we free ourselves of any preconceived notions regarding what must be for the Redemption to come.

The sweetening stage is when our individual messianic spark shines and we are actively engaged in redeeming our particular corner of the world.

3. sweetening	revelation of one's individual spark of the Messiah
2. separation	belief in the imminent coming of the Messiah despite the apparent unreadiness of the world
1. submission	anxiety over the Messiah's delay

11
Therapy and Spiritual Paths

THE MESSIANIC PATH

Since its inception in the 18th century, the Hassidic movement has been re-focusing Jewish consciousness on redemption. The Ba'al Shem Tov wrote in a letter to his brother-in-law[1] that on Rosh Hashanah of the year 1746, he experienced an "ascent of soul" into the spiritual worlds. When he reached the realm where the soul of the Messiah waits to descend into the world, he asked him: "When will you arrive?" The soul of the Messiah responded: "When *your* teachings are spread to the farthest reaches." In other words, through the Ba'al Shem Tov's teachings, the world can and should be prepared to receive the revelations that will accompany the coming of the Messiah.

By gently lifting the veil concealing the new revelations of the Torah that will accompany the messianic era, the Ba'al Shem Tov and his disciples began the subtle and gradual process of shifting the collective focus of the Jewish people from the travails of exile to the anticipation of the Redemption, preparing the world for the new order of consciousness that will be established upon the advent of the Messiah.

When someone would come to join the circle of the Ba'al Shem Tov, the Ba'al Shem Tov would ask him, "What do you remember?" This penetrating question would awaken the new disciple's unconscious and bring up what lay hidden in the recesses of his psyche to his conscious mind. This included all the unresolved issues he had repressed throughout his lifetime, remnants of previous lifetimes, and particularly, the life of his soul before its descent from its abode in heaven into his physical body.[2]

In recalling his soul's "prehistory," his life before birth, the disciple would first remember his soul's origin in the higher worlds. The first dawning of the soul's consciousness was its overwhelming awareness of God's presence. Absorbed in this sublime bliss, the soul aspired to do no more than remain in it.[3] When it remembers this state after having descended into the body, the soul experiences a deep, sublime sense of spiritual submission to God, a desire to be embraced in the bosom of God the way an infant longs for its mother's bosom.

When the time came for the soul to enter the body, it heard God command it to descend into this world to perform His mission and fulfill its unique purpose in life. On the one hand, the challenge excited it;[4] on the other, it was afraid to leave God's protective presence. But it accepted its task on earth of separating good from evil and dedicated itself to strengthening the dominion of good over evil. When the soul remembers the Divine decree to descend into this world in order to perform its mission, this arouses in it a sense of responsibility to achieve its purpose, always differentiating between its true goal and false illusions, separating good from evil.

Finally, the soul descended into this lowest world and was vested in a physical body. Just before its birth, it was administered an oath: "Be righteous, and do not be wicked!"[5] This oath filled it with power and spiritual fortitude, enabling it to withstand the tests of life and successfully fulfill its mission.[6] When it remembers this oath, it draws upon the Divine power channeled through it to sweeten reality.

These three memories of the primal states of consciousness before birth follow the general paradigm of spiritual growth:

3. sweetening	remembering the oath before birth
2. separation	remembering the decree to descend to earth
1. submission	remembering one's soul basking in God's presence

As we shall see, three major streams of Hassidism sprang from the Ba'al Shem Tov's teachings. The three stages of human primal memory underlie the inter-relationship between these three paths and the psychologies of the three types of Jews.

THREE STREAMS

The Talmud divides the Jewish people into three categories: righteous, wicked, and intermediate. In the *Tanya*, the seminal work of *Chabad* Hassidism, Rabbi Shneur Zalman analyzes the psychologies of these three types based on the relative dominance of their opposing inclinations toward good and evil:

- the *tzadik* (the "righteous") is someone who has overcome and uprooted his urge to do evil,

- the *rasha* (the "wicked") has succumbed to his urge to do evil, and

- the *beinoni* (the "intermediate") has not uprooted his urge to do evil but holds it in check.

The *tzadik*, Rabbi Shneur Zalman points out, is a most rare phenomenon. Only in exceptional instances may someone who has actualized his or her full potential to become a *beinoni* become a *tzadik*. Therefore, the ideal of the *beinoni* is the one most of us are working toward.[7] Indeed, the *Tanya* is subtitled "The Book of the Intermediates."

But by subtitling his work "The Book of the Intermediates," Rabbi Shneur Zalman implies that there must also be a "Book of the Wicked" and a "Book of the Righteous."[8] The Hassidic "Book of the Wicked" must instruct those of us who are far from God how to return to Him. The Hassidic "Book of the Righteous" must teach us what it means to be a *tzadik* and how to become one.

In one sense, the *Tanya* itself comprises its own "Book of the Wicked" and "Book of the Righteous." Inasmuch as the "intermediate" is someone situated between the two extremes of wicked and righteous, one foot stepping out of the world of the wicked and one foot stepping into the world of the righteous, the "Book of the Intermediate" must describe the ontologies of the wicked and the righteous, as well. The *Tanya* thus begins with the words of the oath quoted above: "...be a *tzadik*, and be not a *rasha*, and even if the whole world tells you that you are a *tzadik*, consider yourself a *rasha*." The very essence of the *beinoni* is the tension between these two antithetical states, *tzadik* and *rasha*.

In particular, the third section of the *Tanya*, *Igeret HaTeshuvah* ("The Letter on Repentance," also known as the "little *Tanya*") is the "Book of the Wicked," which guides the estranged soul in its return to God. The fourth section of the *Tanya*, *Igeret HaKodesh* ("The Holy Letter"), is the "Book of the Righteous"; it teaches us how to arouse God's mercy on His people by having mercy on our fellow Jew through righteous and charitable acts. This is the principle focus of the *tzadik*'s life.[9]

In the larger context of the Hassidic movement, it is said among Hassidim that the classic work of Rabbi Nachman of Breslov, *Likutei Moharan*, is the Hassidic "Book of the Wicked." Even those who have fallen to the lowest depth will identify with Rabbi Nachman's consoling and encouraging words and be inspired by them to return to God and approach Him in heartfelt prayer.

The Hassidic "Book of the Righteous" is said to be the classic *Noam Elimelech*, by Rabbi Elimelech of Lizhensk.[10] In it, Rabbi Elimelech shows how the Torah instructs us in the subtle nuances of the spiritual work of *tzadikim*, the shepherds of the people of Israel, who, in their consummate love of God and His people, reach up to Him and bring down His blessings down upon them. One might even say that *Noam Elimelech* is the "handbook" of *tzadikim*.

The different spiritual approaches to life of the *rasha*, the *beinoni*, and the *tzadik* align with the Ba'al Shem Tov's three stages of spiritual growth, submission, separation, and sweetening, respectively:

The path of Rabbi Nachman of Breslov is directed toward people who feel themselves caught in the clutches of their evil inclination, unable to escape. The advice he offers and the mode of behavior he develops are intended mainly to keep such people from despairing over their situation. He encourages them to pour out their hearts to God in solitude and express to Him in detail all their anxieties and problems, to devote much time to reciting psalms and prayers, and to cultivate simple humility and submission before the Creator.[11] This maintains their awareness that God is with them at all times, no matter what they have done, and that they can always call upon Him and connect with Him through prayer.[12]

Rabbi Shneur Zalman advises aspiring "intermediates" to ignore their anxieties. Their ongoing battle is to distinguish between good and evil at deeper and deeper levels of their psyche and identify with the good. While fully recognizing their inner evil and feeling attacked by it from time to time, they push away evil by ignoring it and draw near good by filling the soul's three modes of expression—thought, speech, and deed—solely with good.

Inasmuch as they have not entirely overcome their ego-based urges and extricated themselves from their desire to indulge in the forbidden, "intermediates" are not ready to face their darker side with the conscious intention of transforming darkness into light. Indeed, they may never reach this level. Still, by ignoring their anxieties, actively filling their minds with wholesome thoughts, and speaking and acting out of loving-kindness, they will eventually neutralize any harmful aspects of their subconscious and ensure that their faculties of thought, word, and deed remain pure and potent in their positive effect on reality. This, in general, is the work of separation.

Rabbi Elimelech encourages his disciples to articulate their anxieties in order to sweeten them.[13] He details how the role of the *tzadik*, having overcome and uprooted his urge to do evil, is to sweeten the evil in those who seek his counsel and transform it into good. This is particularly true of the *tzadik* who assumes the mantle of leadership as a *rebbe*. The complete transformation of evil into good at the hands of the consummate Hassidic master is the fullest expression of the vision of the Ba'al Shem Tov.[14]

In the teachings of this stream of Hassidism, the more people recognize and appreciate the exalted spiritual stature of the *tzadik*, the more will they be devoted to him. They do not need to confront their inner evil alone, for the holiness of the *tzadik* envelops them and neutralizes their darker side, enabling them to establish a true and profound connection to God. In *Noam Elimelech*, Rabbi Elimelech guides Hassidic masters and those who follow[15] and emulate them in the ultimate hope of joining their ranks.[16]

To use the imagery of war and peace, the life-task of the *rasha* is to enlist in the army of God; the life-task of the *beinoni* is to wage the wars of God; the life-task of the *tzadik*, who comes from a place of inner peace, is to *peacefully* achieve Divine victory[17] and bring peace to the world.

MATURATION IN THERAPY

We can view the three major streams of Hassidism as stages in our ongoing, maturing therapy or spiritual development, which are additionally reflected in the successive stages of our lives.

The approach of Breslov is the underlying bedrock of the spiritual life. The type of advice we find in Rabbi Nachman's teachings is particularly suited to the "adolescent" stage of spiritual life, when we are concerned with consolidating our own sense of identity.[18] When we find ourselves tossed by the tempest of our own turbulent emotional development, we need most to hear that God loves us and is there with us, even in the depths to which we occasionally fall. We need most to remember how we enjoyed God's protective presence before we descended into this world.[19] When our spiritual immaturity makes us reluctant to face our problems directly, we can be inspired by this memory, take refuge in God, stand before Him in submission, and pour out our souls to Him in heartfelt prayer.

This reliance on God as our loving, understanding, forgiving parent expresses the intrinsic connection between His essence and ours.[20] Although this connection may make us feel comfortable airing our conscious anxieties and converse freely with God as with a loving mentor, our relatively immature understanding of ourselves prevents us from probing our deeper and more concealed levels of evil. They remain hidden in the unconscious, threatening to surface in the future.

The spiritual system of the *Tanya* is suited to those of us who have matured into spiritual "adulthood" and are ready to know the full extent of our darker side (without yet combating it directly). Our intellectual detachment at this stage allows us to view evil in its proper perspective and referee a balanced and honest interplay between our higher aspirations (arising from our Divine soul) and our human frailty (arising from our animal soul). Having matured sufficiently to recognize our unique purpose in life, we identify the evil within us as that which prevents us from fulfilling our mission. Although the evil is indeed within us, hindering our progress, we know that, in truth, it is not who we are. At this stage of spiritual maturity, it is paramount that we recall that our Divine souls were given a holy task and an enemy to fight and subdue.

When we dissociate ourselves from our own evil, we can engage in a broad, deep intellectual analysis of all facets of our psyche and the role they play in our connection to God. This type of analysis has been developed most fully in the extensive literature of the *Chabad* tradition.

Out of this honest recognition of our human capacities— and their detailed intellectual analysis—springs the potential for each of us to behave as a *tzadik* of sorts.[21] Our analysis enables us to see that all the shortcomings in the world, even those in ourselves, exist only for our elevation. We can become aware of the evil hidden away in our soul and reveal it to the objective "other" within ourselves (our higher self, the potential *tzadik* within) or to our counselor. In this fashion, we find the way to rectify and elevate the evil and transform it into good. Eventually, we are able to assume the role of the counselor for others and act as the fully mature and wise elder whose experience in life has granted him the insight of the sage. At this stage of spiritual development, we feel the Divine power granted us when we were adjured to "be righteous, and not wicked!"

We now can see how our concept of evil changes with our stage of spiritual maturity. At the first level, we see evil as whatever the Torah defines as wrongdoing and as our inclination to do wrong. At the second level, evil becomes the psychological complexes that block us from fulfilling our purpose in life. At the third level, we identify evil as the traumas, trials, and tribulations of this lifetime and past lifetimes. Here, whatever is bitter is evil, and its very existence is meant to motivate us to sweeten it by transforming it into good. What stifled our development earlier now spurs us on, and "evil [becomes] the throne of good."[22]

stage of spiritual development	stage in life	attitude toward evil
3. sweetening	full maturity	a challenge to be sweetened
2. separation	adulthood	psychological complexes
1. submission	childhood and adolescence	objective wrong

THE APEX OF THE ARC

The middle of the nine sub-stages of submission, separation, and sweetening is the fifth, separation within separation. We identified this stage as self-redefinition—the renewal of Divine consciousness at its source—and the technique we described to achieve this end was meditative prayer.

When we discussed the dynamics of meditative prayer, we noted that according to Kabbalah, the liturgy describes the ascent of the soul to its source and its subsequent descent back into created reality. In the larger context of all nine sub-stages, we may view all the stages preceding meditative prayer as techniques that help us up and out of our problems, and all those following it as techniques that help us descend back into reality in order to face and rectify our problems. Meditative prayer thus becomes the apex of the ascent and descent that describes the arc of the entire therapeutic process.

Seen this way, meditative prayer is not the midpoint of the therapeutic process but its high point, its goal; not the means to an end but the end itself. Indeed, the purpose of transforming evil into good, the end of the process, is to free us to realize our true, Divine selves and unite with God in the most profound and meaningful way. Meditative prayer is thus the epitome of actualized Divinity. As the sages said, "would that a person pray the whole day."[23] The Ba'al Shem Tov described consummate spiritual maturity as the ability to sustain conscious union with God even while engaged in mundane conversation with another person.

We have identified the stage of separation with the Hassidic path of the *Chabad* school. And indeed, meditative prayer is accorded a central role in the classic *Chabad* lifestyle. Seasoned adherents to this path become practiced at long, deliberate prayer that often extends for hours on end. The deep, intricate discourses on Kabbalistic doctrine that characterize *Chabad* literature become the subject of intense meditation before and during prayers (especially on Shabbat), as the individual veteran of life elevates all his worldly experience in his upward communion with his inner self and his Creator.

THE SWEETENING WITHIN SWEETENING OF THE *BEINONI* AND THE *TZADIK*

We have associated the three stages of submission, separation, and sweetening with the three psychological prototypes of *rasha*, *beinoni*, and *tzadik*, respectively. In this context, sweetening seems to lie only within the province of the *tzadik*. After all, only someone totally divorced from evil can safely transform someone else's evil into good. Since the ideal of the *beinoni* is the one most of us are working toward and the highest type of spiritual psyche we can achieve on our own, it would appear that most of us are incapable of progressing beyond the separation stage.

True, we may assume the role of the *tzadik* in a relative, limited sense, concomitant with our spiritual maturity. This is especially true as we approach the messianic redemption and are empowered by our dawning messianic consciousness, as we have explained above. But in an absolute sense, most of us cannot honestly expect to transform our inner negativities into good so consummately that we never again experience even the slightest urge to fall prey to them—this being the definition of a *tzadik*. The most we may hope is to be counseled either by a *tzadik*, someone profoundly inspired by a *tzadik*, or a "relative" *tzadik* (even ourselves) and thereby transform some of our inner darkness into light.

If we look a little closer, however, we see that the way we have described the Kabbalistic psychotherapeutic process requires no more of us—even at the consummate level of sweetening within sweetening—than is required of anyone aspiring to be a *beinoni*. It is possible for anyone to transform evil into good at the behavioral level—including the most sublime form of behavior, thought.[24] Even though we may not be able to reach and root out the inner negativity of our psyches, we can purify our behavior and commit ourselves to a new way of life through positive reinterpretation of our anxieties and their causes. Thus, any of us can aspire to follow the full therapeutic path to psychological well-being and enjoy its full benefits.

What then, is sweetening within sweetening for a *tzadik*?

To answer this question, let us note that Rabbi Shneur Zalman differentiates between two types of *tzadik*: the partial *tzadik* and the complete *tzadik*. The partial *tzadik* has annihilated his inner evil to the point where he no longer feels any dark urges, but not so completely that he feels utterly foreign to it. Evil does not threaten him, but it does not overly upset him, either. He has passed the moral divide between *beinoni* and *tzadik*, but he is still in the process of separating himself from his inner evil.

The complete *tzadik*, in contrast, has so dissociated himself from evil that it has no place in his universe. He is truly consumed with the messianic anxiety we described above: the existence of even the smallest iota of evil is for him an issue of the utmost gravity, an existential crisis of cosmic proportions. He has sweetened his inner evil so completely that not even the faintest trace of it remains.

Thus, we may summarize the inter-inclusion of sweetening with sweetening as follows:

sweetening within sweetening	3. sweetening	evil has been transformed into good	complete *tzadik*
	2. separation	evil is in the process of being transformed into good	partial *tzadik*
	1. submission	evil behavior has been replaced by good	*beinoni*

Upon even closer examination, we find that Rabbi Shneur Zalman further describes in the *Tanya*[25] three stages in the spiritual life of the complete *tzadik*. He experiences submission when he annihilates the evil within him; like King David, he says, "my heart within me is void [of evil],"[26] "for he has killed it by fasting."[27] He experiences separation when he consummately dissociates himself from and hates evil. He experiences sweetening when his inner evil has been totally transformed into good.

To summarize:

sweetening within sweetening within sweetening	3. sweetening	transformation of evil into good	complete *tzadik*
	2. separation	hatred of evil	
	1. submission	annihilation of evil	

12
The Therapeutic Books
of the Bible

THREE UNIQUE BOOKS

Although all the books of the Bible are rich with insights into human nature, three books may be considered the quintessential "psychological" books of the Bible: the Book of Psalms, the Book of Proverbs, and the Book of Job.

The Hebrew text of the Bible is annotated with diacritical symbols, known as cantillation marks, that indicate how the text is to be sung. Since they indicate both the melody to be used for each word and the overall cadence of the verse, these marks are both a musical shorthand and a guideline to the grammatical structure of the text.

The same system of cantillation marks is employed for all the books of the Bible, with the exception of these three books. Their unique system is more complex than the regular system and is also harder to chant. Almost all Jewish communities have lost the knowledge of the melodies represented by this system of cantillation.

The fact that these three books are crafted and chanted in a complicated and somewhat esoteric way sets them apart from the other books of the Bible, as if they reflect a more complex and penetrating way of experiencing life. This notion is reinforced by their overtly deep, philosophical content, which distinguishes them from the other legal and narrative literature that makes up the Bible.

Upon close examination, we may parallel these three books with the three stages of spiritual growth and Kabbalistic psychotherapy we have been discussing. The order in which these books appear in the Bible follows this developmental sequence.

3. sweetening	articulating anxiety	Job
2. separation	ignoring anxiety	Proverbs
1. submission	suppressing anxiety	Psalms

The Book of Psalms gives full expression to our soul's prayers to God. For thousands of years, Jews have recited psalms to voice the emotions of their broken hearts in times of pain and suffering, to arouse God's mercy and to thank Him for the miracles He has shown them.

The Book of Psalms was written by King David, "the pleasant singer of Israel."[1] King David, the quintessential king, personified the ideal of rectified ego, humility, and submission. When David's wife Michal derided him for undignified behavior after he danced before the ark of the covenant in full view of the public, he replied: "I shall behave even more humbly than this, and I shall be lowly in my own eyes..."[2] By virtue of his humility before God and his subjects, King David was granted the strength and conviction that enabled him to lead his people fearlessly, with the authority befitting a ruler of Israel.

King David taught us by his own example that it is always possible to return to God.[3] When we recite psalms, we identify with King David and, no matter how far away we may feel from God, the psalms uplift our spirits and restore our hope.

The Book of Proverbs, written by King Solomon, is the book of Divine ethics. Rashi,[4] the classic Torah commentator, writes in the beginning of his commentary to this book:

> All [King Solomon's] statements are parables and analogies. He compares the Torah to a good woman and idolatry to a harlot.... He used these analogies in order to teach man wisdom and ethics, that he might dedicate himself to the study of the Torah, which is the true wisdom, ethics, and understanding.

In the Book of Proverbs, the wise father counsels his son how to escape the evil inclination. The advice he gives is to replace the thoughts planted by the evil inclination with thoughts about the beauty of the Torah, which is compared to a good woman:

> Let your fountain be blessed; and rejoice with the wife of your youth.... And why should you, my son, be infatuated with a strange woman, and embrace the bosom of an alien?[5]

This advice is that of the therapeutic process of separation, in which we excise dark thoughts from the mind by replacing them with positive thoughts. We replace the "strange woman," the egocentric thoughts that enter our mind, with a truly "beautiful woman," the wisdom of the Torah.

The third of these three books, the Book of Job, is a virtual manual of psychology, describing in detail the process of psychoanalysis.

Job's physical suffering engenders a psychological anxiety, an existential pain that he cannot bear. When he is first confronted with this pain, he behaves like a disconsolate mourner, unable to voice his feelings. He sits silently for a long time in the presence of his three friends, Eliphaz, Bildad, and Zophar, who come to visit and comfort him, but who finally blame him for his own troubles. They each attempt to administer a different form of therapy to him and to convince him that his suffering is not without cause.

Job does not blaspheme God, but he does not accept his suffering as justified, either. He is therefore unable to accept what happened to him with love and submission before God. Unable to cope with his pain, the first words he speaks are to curse the day he was born.

After his three friends' unsuccessful attempt to comfort him, a fourth figure speaks, the young Elihu. In deference to his elders, Elihu had remained silent throughout the preceding dialogues. He now offers his sensitive but convincing analysis, spoken out of honest, unaffected concern. He prefaces his remarks by saying, "I thought that age would speak, and the passage of years would impart wisdom," but when he saw that the others could not answer Job's questions, he became disillusioned with the elders and concluded that "rather, it is man's spirit and God's soul [within him] that gives him understanding."[6]

Elihu is disillusioned with the elders' inability to truly empathize with Job's pain and comfort him with words spoken from the depth of their hearts. In their need to justify God's actions, they only seem able to blame Job. In response, Job transfers (in the terminology of conventional psychology) his painful, angry feelings against God, which he had never verbalized, to his three would-be analysts. But when Elihu speaks, truly empathizing with Job, he awakens Job's inner love for God, which, though hidden, is ever present in the unconscious root of the Divine soul. Elihu, a true *tzadik*, makes himself transparent, and so Job's dialogue with Elihu spontaneously segues into a dialogue with God. When God Himself responds to Job, he recovers, both psychologically and physically, and even surpasses his initial state of health and well-being.

Elihu's ability to advise Job in a meaningful way comes from Divine inspiration, which can rest on a young person as easily as on an elder.[7] In the process of Kabbalistic psychotherapy, Divine inspiration will rest upon the therapist if he truly loves and empathizes with his patient. Only with God's help can the therapist hope to penetrate the depths of his patient's unconscious and thereby help him or her solve his psychological problems.

THE MESSIAH AS PSYCHOLOGIST

Elihu, who begins the process of true healing, plays both the role of Elijah the prophet, the harbinger of the Redemption, as well as that of the Messiah.[8] In consoling Job, he plays the role of Elijah, preparing Job for the true therapy he is about to administer, the redemption to come. Then, by administering the therapy, he untangles the twisted knots of Job's psyche, preparing him for God's revelation, just as the Messiah will heal the world and prepare it to receive the new revelations of God's Torah.

The Messiah will be the consummate psychologist, who will unravel all the convoluted nightmares of our bitter exiles and reveal their good inner core. He will know how to open us up and enable us to articulate our anxieties. He will gather all the scattered fragments of our shattered souls and bring these fragments back to the inner, pure kernel which was always true to God. He will remind humanity of its forgotten identity, and thereby solve the riddle of our psychological malaise.

This is the psychological dimension of the Messiah's task of gathering the dispersed of Israel back to Zion. In the Kabbalah, Zion (in Hebrew, *Tzion*, which means "point" or "marker") signifies the innermost point of every Jewish heart, while the exile of the Jewish people from their homeland symbolizes the scattered consciousness of all who have lost touch with their inner being.

Nachmanides,[9] the great Talmudist and Kabbalist, explains that Elihu succeeded where his three predecessors failed because he was able to penetrate the depths of Job's soul and remind him of all he had forgotten—not only during his own lifetime but also in all his previous incarnations. According to this interpretation, one of the paramount aspects of psychological therapy that the Book of Job teaches us is the contribution of reincarnation to each individual's present mentality and psychological condition. All previous incarnations are recorded on our unconscious; our previous lifetimes are the fossilized strata of our present unconscious minds. Hence, for us to heal, it is necessary for our counselor to take into consideration our soul's experiences in previous incarnations.

To do this, our counselor does not necessarily have to possess the prophetic insight required to know our previous incarnations. He must simply be aware that by delving deeper and deeper into our unconscious mind, he is tracing a path through our previous incarnations, healing wounds inflicted during our past lifetimes. By reducing all anxieties and wounds to their most basic form, he will eventually arrive at their origin in the primordial sin and the origin of our soul in the comprehensive soul of Adam.[10] That is when healing is assured.

(For this reason, we are taught that the name *Adam* in Hebrew is an acronym for the three individuals whose lives exemplify the dynamic of fall-repentance-redemption: *A*dam, *D*avid, and the *M*essiah.)

At the end of the Book of Job, God Himself addresses Job and unfolds all the mysteries of creation before him. In the final analysis, Job merits this revelation of the Torah's secrets because of all the anxiety he has suffered. His suffering, both psychological and physical, brings him into full consciousness of the greatness of God and the smallness of man. The end of his journey recalls the end of the Book of Ecclesiastes: "The end of the matter, all having been heard, is: fear God and keep His commandments, for this is the whole of man."[11]

THE ASCENT THROUGH THE SOUL

Job's ascent through psychotherapy, facilitated by his five partners in dialogue, Eliphaz, Bildad, Zophar, Elihu, and God, corresponds to the five levels of the soul described in Kabbalah.

The first three friends correspond to the three levels of the soul that are invested in the body and therefore limited by its parameters: the animating power of the soul (*nefesh* or "creature"), the emotions (*ruach* or "spirit"), and the intellect (*neshamah* or "breath"). These levels of the soul are incapable on their own of solving the problems that surface from a person's subconscious. The fourth friend, Elihu, corresponds to the fourth level of the soul, the will (*chayah* or "living being"). Though it acts upon the body, the will is not localized within it, and thus is partially free from the constraints imposed on the lower levels of the soul.

God's revelation to Job corresponds to the fifth, highest level of the soul (*yechidah* or "unique one"), the source of the soul within God Himself.

God	*yechidah*	"unique one"	source of soul in God
Elihu	*Chayah*	"living being"	super-rational will
Zophar	*Neshamah*	"breath"	intellect
Bildad	*Ruach*	"spirit"	emotions
Eliphaz	*Nefesh*	"creature"	animating power

The psychological odyssey of Job is thus the revelation of deeper and higher aspects of the soul, accomplished by its successive release from the limitations of the body. (The idea that by engaging in a dialogue with a counselor or therapist we can divest ourselves of various psychological problems and address the strata of the psyche being exposed one after another is documented extensively in psychological literature.)

The process of talking with oneself as mirrored in another person helps along the therapeutic process. Although Job's three friends do not solve his problem, they serve as a springboard for the next levels. In this sense, the three friends exemplify the three meanings of the Hebrew verb in the verse from Proverbs: "If there be anxiety in a man's heart let him suppress/ignore/articulate it...," while the responses of Elihu and God correspond to the "good word" that turns the anxiety "into joy."

Still, despite the psychological healing that is possible through the process we have outlined in our study, the ultimate key to unraveling and healing the world will only be available to us when the Messiah comes. Until then, in the words of the Talmud, "we can understand neither the tranquility of the wicked nor the suffering of the righteous."[12] Certainly we cannot hope to understand all the terrible tragedies that have befallen the Jewish people, and, indeed, all people. Only when the Messiah, the consummate psychologist, comes, will we be able to discern the good hidden within all the apparent evil. For then, for all time, darkness will turn into light and bitterness into sweetness.

Glossary

Note: all foreign terms are Hebrew. Terms preceded by an asterisk have their own entries.

Anxiety: As used in this book, "anxiety" means a fear or a feeling of apprehension whether in the presence or absence of a specific threat.

Ba'al Shem Tov ("Master of the Good Name [of God]"): title of Rabbi Yisrael ben Eliezer (1698-1760), founder of the Hassidic movement (*Hassidism).

Beinoni **("intermediate")**: someone who possesses an evil urge but controls it and does not sin. There are many levels of *beinonim*, from the one who is in a continuous conscious state of battle in order to overcome his evil inclination, to the one so engrossed in his Divine service of Torah and *mitzvot* that he is virtually unaware of the evil inclination dormant in him. See *tzadik*, *rasha*.

Bible: the Pentateuch (the Five Books of Moses: Genesis, Exodus, Leviticus, Numbers, and Deuteronomy); the Prophets (consisting of eight books: Joshua, Judges, Samuel, Kings, Isaiah, Jeremiah, Ezekiel, and the Twelve Prophets); and the Writings (the Hagiographa, consisting of eleven books: Psalms, Proverbs, Job, Ruth, the Song of Songs, Ecclesiastes, Lamentations, Esther, Daniel, Ezra-Nehemiah, and Chronicles).

Bitterness: a deep, existential dissatisfaction with life, born of awareness of our own shortcomings. Bitterness is the middle

147

path between the resignation of self-acceptance and the depression that comes from despairing of ever bettering ourselves.

Chabad: acronym for *chochmah, binah, da'at* ("wisdom, understanding, knowledge"): 1. the first triad of *sefirot* (Divine emanations), which constitute the intellect. 2. the branch of *Hassidism founded by Rabbi Shneur Zalman of Liadi (1745-1812), emphasizing the role of the intellect and meditation in the service of God.

Chashmal: *Chashmal* appears in the first chapter of the Book of Ezekiel as part of the prophet's vision of the Divine chariot. The word *chashmal* may be seen as a compound of the words *chash* ("silent") and *mal* ("severing" or "speaking"). According to Kabbalah, it is a type of spiritual light or energy originating in the Divine oneness above time and space, the experience of the "soft, silent voice" heard by the prophet Elijah. In the creative process, it becomes personified as a genre of angels that are "sometimes silent and sometimes speak." When we include the alternate meaning of *mal*, "severing," the word indicates the threefold process of spiritual growth (submission, separation, and sweetening).

Chayah ("living one"): the second highest of the five levels of the *soul.

Depression: As used in this book, "depression" means sadness, melancholy, or despondency. In extreme cases, depression may cause impaired social and/or physiological functioning.

Drug therapy: treatment of psychological health problems through chemical medications.

Ego: As used in this book, "ego" means one's self-orientation or self-consciousness.

Egocentric: self-oriented, selfish, self-interested.

Egoistic: exaggeratedly conscious of oneself.

Evil: As used in this book, "evil" is whatever contravenes Divine consciousness. This includes whatever the Torah defines as wrongdoing, our inclination to do wrong, the psychological complexes that block us from fulfilling our purpose in life, and the traumas, trials, and tribulations of this lifetime and past lifetimes.

In the imagery of Kabbalah, evil is likened to a shell or peel that holds the "kernel" or "fruit"—the Divine spark—captive within it.

Farbrengen: a Hassidic gathering.

Garments (of the soul): means of expression (whether to oneself or to others): thought, speech, and action.

Hassidism (from *chesed*, "loving-kindness"): 1. An attribute or way of life that goes beyond the letter of the law. 2. The movement within Judaism founded by Rabbi Yisrael Ba'al Shem Tov (1648-1760), the purpose of which is to awaken the Jewish people to its own inner self through the inner dimension of the Torah and thus to prepare the way for the advent of the Messiah. 3. The written and oral teachings of this movement.

Inter-inclusion: the inclusion of the nature or mentality of all members of a set in each member of the set. The Kabbalistic "holographic" principle, characteristic of everything holy.

Kabbalah ("received tradition"): the esoteric dimension of the Torah.

Likutei Moharan ("Collected [Teachings of] Rabbi Nachman"): compendium of teachings of Rabbi Nachman of Breslov (1772-1810).

Meditation: The correct meaning of this word is "contemplating a subject in depth." Meditation is a cognitive endeavor, not a technique intended to *rid* the mind of thought. Clearing the mind of mental interference is a prerequisite for meditation.

Messiah ("anointed one"): the prophesied descendant of King David who will reinstate the Torah-ordained monarchy (which he will head), rebuild the Holy *Temple, and gather the exiled Jewish people to their homeland. This series of events (collectively called "the *Redemption") will usher in an era of eternal, universal peace and true knowledge of God, called "the *messianic era."

Messianic era: the era of eternal, universal peace and true knowledge of God that will be ushered in by the *Messiah.

Narcissism: conceit, excessive love or admiration of oneself. In extreme cases, narcissism entails erotic pleasure in contemplating oneself, generally involving a regression to an infantile stage of development.

Nefesh **("creature," "soul")**: the lowest of the five levels of the *soul.

Ne'ilah **("locking")**: the closing prayer of *Yom Kippur.

Neshamah **("soul")**: the third of the five levels of the *soul.

Noam Elimelech **("The Sweetness of Elimelech")**: A compendium of the Hassidic teachings of Rabbi Elimelech of Lizhensk.

Paranoia: As used in this book, "paranoia" means exaggerated fear or distrust of others or circumstances, feeling threatened by them, or feeling pursued by them.

Phobia: a persistent, irrational fear that is out of proportion to the real danger and that makes the individual avoid the object of his or her fear.

Psyche: the *soul. The "abode" of the psyche is the conscious mind.

Psychoanalysis: As used in this book, "psychoanalysis" means the administration of psychotherapy by a counselor. Classical psychoanalysis is the method of psychotherapy first developed by Dr. Sigmund Freud to treat psychological malaises by attempting to penetrate and explore the subconscious and deal with repressed anxieties and conflicts.

Psychotherapy: Any method for curing psychological ills through psychological techniques (as opposed to chemical remedies). Common forms of conventional psychotherapy include behavior therapy, cognitive psychotherapy, and group psychotherapy.

Rasha **("wicked one")**: one who succumbs to his urge to do evil and commits a sin. He retains this status until he regrets his deeds and mends his behavior.

Rebbe ("teacher"): 1. a term used to describe or address a teacher of Torah. 2. leader of a branch of the Hassidic movement.

Redemption: the series of events that usher in the *messianic era.

Repression: see *suppression.

Rosh Hashanah: ("beginning of the year"): the Jewish New Year, commemorating the creation of man on the sixth day of creation; a day of universal judgment.

Ruach **("spirit")**: the second level of the *soul.

Sages: as used in this book, the sages of the Talmudic period, whose words are recorded in the Talmud, the Midrash, and the *Zohar*.

Separation: identifying the good and evil in any particular entity or situation; the second phase of spiritual growth as taught by the Ba'al Shem Tov.

Soul: the animating life or consciousness within man (or any other creature, see *Sha'ar HaYichud VehaEmunah*, ch. 1). The Jew possesses an additional *"Divine soul" which is focused on God's concerns in creation.

The essence of the soul possesses five manifestations ("names" or levels), as follows:

name (level)		experience
yechidah	"unique one"	unity with God
chayah	"living being"	awareness of God as continually creating the world
neshamah	"breath"	vitality of intelligence
ruach	"spirit"	vitality of emotion
nefesh	"creature"	physical vitality

Soul, animal: the soul that drives us toward material or spiritual self-preservation and toward enhancing our material or sensual enjoyment.

Soul, Divine: the soul that drives us toward God and submission to His will.

Subconscious: In classical psychology, this term includes the unconscious and preconscious. In popular usage (and in this book), the term is used as a synonym for the *unconscious.

Submission: subduing the ego; the first of the three stages of spiritual growth as taught by the Ba'al Shem Tov.

Suppression: In classical psychology, "suppression" means conscious exclusion of unacceptable desires, thoughts, or memories from the mind, in contrast to *repression*, which means unconscious exclusion of such desires, thoughts, or memories from the mind. In this work, we use the term *repression* to refer to both the conscious and subconscious processes, and reserve the term *suppression* for the subdual of the ego, this being the first meaning of King Solomon's advice for dealing with anxiety, aligned with "submission," the first of phase of the Ba'al Shem Tov's threefold process of spiritual growth.

Sweetening: revealing the inner core of goodness within evil and transforming whatever possible of the evil into good— "transforming darkness into light"; the third stage of spiritual growth as taught by the Ba'al Shem Tov.

***Tanya* ("It has been taught")**: the seminal work of *Chabad *Hassidism, written by Rabbi Shneur Zalman of Liadi (1745-1812). Also known as *Likutei Amarim* ("Collected Teachings") and *Sefer shel Beinonim* ("The Book of the Intermediates").

Temple: (or "Holy Temple"; Hebrew: *Beit HaMikdash*, "house of the sanctuary"): the central sanctuary in Jerusalem which serves as the physical abode of the indwelling of God's Presence on earth and as the venue for the sacrificial service. The Temple is the focal point of one's spiritual consciousness. The first Temple was built by King Solomon (833 BCE) and destroyed by the Babylonians (423 BCE); the second Temple was built by Zerubabel (synonymous, according to some opinions, with Nehemiah, 353 BCE), remodeled by Herod and destroyed by the Romans (68 CE); the third, eternal Temple will be built by the *Messiah.

Torah: ("teaching"): God's will and wisdom as communicated to man. The Torah pre-existed creation, and God used the Torah as His blueprint in creating the world.

God certainly communicated the teachings of the Torah in some form to Adam, who then transmitted them orally from generation to generation. However, God "officially" gave the Torah to mankind c. 1313 BCE (and during the ensuing 40 years) at Mt. Sinai through Moses. The Ten Commandments were pronounced in the presence of the entire Jewish people.

God gave the Torah in two parts: the written Torah and the oral Torah. The written Torah originally consisted of the Five Books of Moses (the "Pentateuch"), the other books being added later (see Bible). The oral Torah was communicated together with the Five Books of Moses as an explanation of the laws and lore included in it. This material was later written down by the sages of the oral Torah in the form of the Talmud, the Midrash, and the *Zohar*.

Tzadik: "righteous" person: someone who has fully overcome the evil inclination of his animal soul (and converted its potential into good). See *beinoni, rasha*.

Unconscious: the repository of thoughts in the mind that usually can only be brought into consciousness through some special technique, such as psychotherapy or psychoanalysis.

***Yechidah* ("single one")**: the highest of the five levels of the *soul.

Yom Kippur: ("Day of Atonement"): the holiest day of the Jewish year, marked by fasting and repentance, particularly through confession of sin.

Zohar ("Brilliance"): Part of the oral Torah and the basic text of Kabbalah, recording the mystical teachings of Rabbi Shimon bar Yochai (2nd century).

Endnotes

Preface

[1] *Zohar* 1:116b. See *Likutei Sichot*, vol. 15, pp. 42 ff.

[2] Isaiah 11:9.

[3] Counting from the first year of creation, which is the year 3760 BCE in the Western calendar.

[4] *Ashmoret HaBoker ad loc.*

[5] *Ba'al Shem Tov* is Rabbi Yisrael's epithet (not his last name), and means "Master of the Good Name [of God]." Thus, Rabbi Yisrael Ba'al Shem Tov is often referred to simply as "the Ba'al Shem Tov."

[6] In the Chabad school of Hassidism, this refers to *Torah Or* (1837) and *Likutei Torah* (1848) (*Likutei Sichot, loc. cit*). These two books are Rabbi Shneur Zalman of Liadi's major exposition of his system of Jewish mystical thought after his seminal work, *Tanya.* See below, endnote 9 to chapter 11.

Likutei Torah is essentially the second volume of *Torah Or,* and would have been published right after it, were it not for a government ban on publishing Jewish books.

[7] Dr. Sigmund Freud (1856-1939) developed the techniques and theories of psychoanalysis in the 1890's. "No historical or sociological account of scientific progress can adequately explain the sudden appearance of psychoanalysis and its discoveries of unconscious psychological processes" (Morton Hunt, *The Story of Psychology* [New York: Doubleday, 1993], p. 174-5).

[8] See also *The Mystery of Marriage*, pp. 378-79, footnotes 19 and 21.

[9] The reason for this disparity within conventional psychology will be explained in chapter 1.

There are different schools of thought within Kabbalah and Hassidism, as well. However, as we will note in chapter 11, these schools correspond to different stages in psychological and spiritual growth, and therefore complement one another.

[10] In Hassidic writings, Hassidism is sometimes referred to as "the Kabbalah of the Ba'al Shem Tov" (the third general revelation of the

teachings of Kabbalah, following and building upon "the Kabbalah of Rabbi Moshe Cordovero" and "the Kabbalah of Rabbi Yitzchak Luria").

Chapter 1

[1] See *Mishneh Torah, De'ot*, ch. 4.

[2] The Ba'al Shem Tov often prescribed dietary and herbal remedies for psychological illnesses.

[3] The teachings of Kabbalah, which form the foundation of Hassidic thought and philosophy, were recast into the psychological terms of human experience primarily by the founder of the Hassidic movement, Rabbi Yisrael Ba'al Shem Tov (1698-1760), his successor Rabbi Dovber, the Maggid of Mezritch (?-1772), and by Rabbi Shneur Zalman of Liadi (1745-1812), the author of the *Tanya*, the seminal work of *Chabad* Hassidism.

[4] "A good wife is one's best friend" (*Mishlei Yisrael* 588). The Torah refers to one's wife as "the woman of your bosom" (Deuteronomy 13:7), i.e., the one closest to your heart; see *The Mystery of Marriage*, ch. 8.

[5] Most recently, the Lubavitcher *Rebbe* has re-emphasized the need for everyone to maintain an ongoing relationship with a Hassidic counselor (*mashpia*). The Hassidic counseling relationship is based on the sages' instruction to "appoint yourself a mentor" (*Avot* 1:6, 16). See, at length, *Panim el Panim*.

[6] That is, as outlined in Maimonides' Thirteen Principles of Faith, and as extended in the teachings of Kabbalah and Hassidism (see *Emunah uMuda'ut*, pp. 185 ff).

[7] The words "know yourself" were inscribed on the shire of the oracle of Apollo in ancient Delphi. Protagoras (c. 485-410 BCE), the first sophist, said, "Man is the measure of all things."

[8] *Berachot* 28b.

[9] 1 Chronicles 28:9.

[10] Genesis 1:27.

[11] Job 19:26.

[12] *Midrash Tanchuma, Naso* 16.

[13] According to Kabbalah, there are four general worlds or levels of consciousness, each of which subdivides into a myriad of individual levels. They are:

world	level of consciousness
Atzilut ("Emanation")	total God-consciousness; no self-awareness
Beriah ("Creation")	potential existence; formless substance
Yetzirah ("Formation")	general existence; archetypes, species
Asiyah ("Action")	particular existence; individual creatures

[14] The normative human psyche is referred to in Kabbalah and Hassidism as the "animal soul" or "vital soul," in contrast to the Divine soul within it.

[15] A true *tzadik* does indeed possess the power to lift another person out of a state of physical or psychological illness (see *Berachot* 5b). This is Divinely-inspired therapy that cures in both the short term and long term.

[16] In the words of the sages: "a prisoner cannot free himself from prison" (*Berachot* 5b). See *Likutei Sichot*, vol. 25, p. 273.

[17] Psalms 139:8.

[18] The mechanism of the escape hatch is Divine mercy, as will be explained later (p. 29).

All that we have said about conventional psychology is not meant to deny, of course, the strides it has made in understanding the normative human psyche, nor its successes in helping people improve their psychological well-being and ability to cope with certain of life's challenges.

In general, Judaism relates positively to secular science and inquiry—as long as they seek to complement and enhance the wisdom of the Torah rather than to supplant or undermine it. Conversely, the wisdom of the Torah can identify what is true and what is not in secular inquiry, and associate each truth with its appropriate context in the Torah's own world-view.

Chapter 2

¹ *Keter Shem Tov* 28.

² See *Keter Shem Tov* 6, where the Ba'al Shem Tov quotes Nachmanides to the effect that in order to choose properly one has to make a conscious effort to first eliminate one's own ulterior motives (that derive from the ego's deceptive self-image).

³ In the *Tanya*, submission and separation are together referred to by the Zoharic term *itkafia* ("suppressing" evil) while sweetening is referred to by the Zoharic term *it'hapcha* ("transforming" evil).

⁴ Genesis 1:1-5.

⁵ We find light referred to in the Bible as being sweet (Ecclesiastes 11:7, "for the light is sweet"). The *Zohar* (1:4a) refers to the transformation of good into evil as "transforming darkness into light and bitterness into sweetness."

⁶ Ezekiel 1:4.

⁷ *Ibid.* 1:4, 1:27, 8:2.

⁸ 1 Kings 19:12.

⁹ *Chagigah* 13b.

¹⁰ Ecclesiastes 3:7.

¹¹ *Keter Shem Tov* 28.

¹² See Rabbi Hillel of Paritch, *Ita biPesikta Rabati*.

¹³ Ecclesiastes 9:17.

Chapter 3

¹ 12:25.

² 1 Kings 5:10.

³ Reading *yash'chenah*—"let him suppress it"—as *yasichenah* [*min hada'at*]—"let him ignore it"—and *yesichenah* [*la'acheirim*]—"let him articulate it [to others]" (*Yoma* 75a).

⁴ in chapters 4 and 6.

⁵ *Sefer HaMa'amarim 5708*, pp. 191-2, 194. Cf. *HaTamim* 239ab (vol. 5, pp. 53-54), *Igrot Kodesh Admur HaRayatz*, vol. 3, p. 438.

⁶ Proverbs 29:13, as interpreted by the sages of the Talmud (*Temurah* 16a).

⁷ Proverbs 24:16.

⁸ *Tanya*, ch. 29 & 33, *Sha'ar HaYichud VehaEmunah*, introduction.

⁹ *Adat Tzadikim*, quoted in *Kol Sipurei Ba'al Shem Tov*, vol. 4, p. 201.

Chapter 4

¹ This is an example of a "long and short path" (pursuing an apparently longer path than necessary to reach the destination in order to effectively penetrate all barriers in the way of reaching the inner, essential point of the goal). See *Malchut Yisrael*, vol. 1, p. 65 ff.

² The story as told here is abridged from Rabbi Adin Steinsaltz, *Beggars and Prayers* (New York: Basic Books, 1979), pp. 113-147.

³ Rabbi Nachman of Breslov (1772-1810) was the great-grandson of the Ba'al Shem Tov.

⁴ See *Tanya*, ch. 26.

⁵ Deuteronomy 4:35.

⁶ *Tanya*, ch. 48 (67b).

⁷ *Notzer Chesed* 4:4.

⁸ See *Shechinah Beineihem*, p. 32 ff, and *Ma'amarei Admur HaZaken—Inyanim*, p. 133. In addition, see *Kuntres HaTefilah*, p. 12-13; *Kuntres HaAvodah* pp. 36-39.

⁹ We will examine the paradox of free will vs. Divine providence in greater detail later on.

¹⁰ *Kalah Rabati* 2:13; *Ketubot* 67a, etc.

¹¹ *Avot* 5:21.

¹² *Kidushin* 82a.

¹³ *Avot* 4:1.

¹⁴ Rabbi Zushya of Anipol (?-1800) was an early Hassidic leader.

¹⁵ Rabbi Mendel Futerfass (1906-1995) was a disciple of the sixth and seventh Lubavitcher *Rebbes*. He was imprisoned in the Soviet Union for his efforts on behalf of Jewish education, and later lived in England

and Israel, where he served until his passing as the elder counselor and mentor at the central Chabad Yeshiva.

[16] As taught by Rabbi Nachman of Breslov.

[17] Psalms 55:23.

[18] p. 37.

[19] *Tanya*, ch. 31. The paradox of the Jew's ability to experience both happiness and "bitterness" simultaneously is posed in the opening lines of *Tanya* and resolved in chapters 26-34.

[20] As we will explain later (p. 127), pouring out our heart privately and verbally to God, our loving and caring Father, is the explicit focus of the Hassidic path of Rabbi Nachman of Breslov.

This practice is most poigniantly expressed in two verses in the Bible: "A prayer of the poor man, when, distraught, he pours out his supplication to God" (Psalms 102:1); "Pour out your heart like water before God" (Lamentations 2:19). This second verse alludes to the stage of "sweetening within submission," for the bitter waters of one's anxious psychological state become sweetened by pouring them out, in faith, before God. The sole appearance of the root "to sweeten" in the Five Books of Moses is when Moses sweetened the bitter waters (Exodus 15:25).

[21] *Yevamot* 64a.

[22] The full story is found in *Me'orot HaGedolim*, cited in *Kol Sipurei Ba'al Shem Tov* 18:5 (vol 3, p. 79; English translation in *Tales of the Ba'al Shem Tov*, vol. 4, p. 54).

[23] *Igeret HaTeshuvah*, ch. 11 (100a).

Chapter 5

[1] Exodus 2:22, 18:3.

[2] *Reishit Chochmah, Anavah* 5, *s.v. Af al pi.*

[3] Deuteronomy 32:9.

[4] *Tanya*, end of ch. 28.

[5] As it is written, "For He stands at the right hand of the destitute, to save him from those who judge his soul" (Psalms 109:31; see *Tanya*, ch. 13 [18a]).

⁶ As we will see later on (p. 106), Rabbi Zushya of Anapoli learned seven positive character traits from a thief, the last of which was never to give up. A thief who does not succeed the first time tries again, and continues to try over and over again. A depressed person has not learned this lesson.

⁷ As we will explain later (p. 132), meditative prayer is the explicit focus of the Hassidic path of Rabbi Shneur Zalman of Liadi, the founder of the Chabad school.

⁸ In Rabbi Nachman of Breslov's tale, "The Master of Prayer," the king's ministers periodically return to their spiritual source in order to renew their power to serve the king.

⁹ The song of each creature is recorded in the Midrash *Perek Shirah*.

¹⁰ *Kuntres HaTefilah* 11.

¹¹ Psalms 34:15, 37:27; cf. *Sotah* 47a; *Sanhedrin* 107b. See below, p. 76.

Positive thinking is the best example of the point we made earlier (p. 24), that one may apply any stage of the ninefold process we are describing here without regard to its order in the sequence. Positive thinking, in its simplest sense—"think good, and it will be good"—is generally the best, most direct response to anxiety. It is placed here, as the sixth step, because we take the power to think positively and the potency of the thought to affect reality from the Torah. In this regard, the previous five steps serve to create the psychological conditions most conducive to contemplating and integrating the truth of the Torah into one's consciousness, as will be explained.

¹² According to the Ba'al Shem Tov (*Keter Shem Tov* 393; see *Likutei Torah* 3:61cd), this equilibrium is the secret of the deepest of the mysteries of the Torah—that of the Red Heifer (Numbers 19), whose ashes purify the impure yet defile the pure. Impurity is the state of consciousness in which one feels "dead," unable to act in the world— i.e., the state of depression. The ashes of the Red Heifer remove the impurity of contact with death; they restore our sense of self-confidence. But since accomplishment always carries with it the danger of self-aggrandizement, the same ashes of the Red Heifer also *defile the pure*.

¹³ *Igrot Kodesh Admor Rayatz*, vol. 2, p. 537; vol. 7, p. 197.

[14] "There is no good but Torah" (*Avodah Zarah* 19b).

[15] Psalms 19:9.

[16] Genesis 37:23.

[17] *Shabbat* 22a; *Bereishit Rabbah* 84:16.

[18] *Bava Kama* 17a, etc.

[19] Proverbs 10:25.

[20] See *Likutei Sichot*, vol. 36, pp. 1 ff.

[21] Deuteronomy 30:15, 19.

[22] See *Lev LaDa'at*, p. 77 ff.

[23] The word in Hebrew for "create" (*bara*) is related to the word for "sound health" (*bari*). The Midrashic statement that God *created* the world through the Torah may therefore be interpreted to mean that God *heals* the world through the Torah; the Torah is the ultimate medicine of creation.

[24] See *Zohar* 1:24a, 2:60a; *Tikunei Zohar* 6; *Tanya*, ch. 3, ch. 23; *Likutei Torah* 4:46a.

[25] p. 48.

[26] *Berachot* 60b.

[27] Indeed, the numerical value in Hebrew of Rabbi Akiva's statement, "Whatever God does is for the good" (611), is identical to that of the word "Torah."

Chapter 6

[1] It is thus explained in Hassidic teachings that the power of speech carries within it a subtle experience of pleasure, and that talking therefore taps the source of pleasure in the soul. Furthermore, we are taught in Kabbalah that pleasure (*ta'anug*) is rooted in faith (*emunah*). Therefore, since speaking enhances our faith in God (as will be explained presently), it augments our experience of pleasure as well.

[2] A "saying of the wise," quoted by the Lubavitcher *Rebbe* in *Igrot Kodesh*, vol. 14, #5047.

[3] As it is written, "as I speak, I believe" (Psalms 116:10). God is described as possessing thirteen attributes of mercy, which are enumerated in Exodus 34:6-7 and begin: "God is merciful and

gracious…." Rabbi Avraham ibn Ezra defines "merciful" to mean that God always foresees our problems (and is so aroused to have mercy on us and guard us), and "gracious" to mean the He always hears us and responds mercifully when we cry out to Him.

⁴ To borrow the terminology of modern physics: transcendence opens one's mind to the possibility of "parallel worlds." In this context, paradoxes such as that of Schrödinger's cat do not pose a threat to the stability of reality. In the terminology of Kabbalah, to ascend to the realm of paradox is to transcend the *tzimtzum* (the initial "contraction" of God's infinite light in order to make "room" for creation) and the "rules of logic" governing the creation that followed it.

⁵ This is a more profound example of a "long and short path" mentioned above (chapter 4, endnote 1).

⁶ *Zohar* 2:163a; see *Tanya*, ch. 9 (14b) and ch. 29 (38a).

⁷ *Zohar* 1:4a.

⁸ See *Siddur Im Dach* 157ab.

⁹ *Tanya*, ch. 26; *Igeret HaKodesh* 11.

¹⁰ Proverbs 3:12.

¹¹ See *Igrot Kodesh* of the Lubavitcher *Rebbe*, vol. 8, #2414, section 5. Quoting the interpretation of the Midrash (*Yalkut Shimoni*, Ecclesiastes 978) on the verse, "He who obeys the commandment will know no evil, and a wise heart will know time and justice" (Ecclesiastes 8:5), the *Rebbe* explains that one who is on the spiritual level of "obeying commandments" "will know no evil," for God, in His mercy, will not reveal concealed evil to him, for he is yet unable to cope with such knowledge. Such knowledge will only confuse and prove harmful to him. In contrast, a person on a higher spiritual level, that of "a wise heart," is prepared to "know time and justice." God reveals to him concealed evil, for he is able to cope with it, to sweeten the evil and transform it into good.

Chapter 7

¹ It is implied in the *Zohar* (3:124b), and so we witness in our generation, that an individual who studies the inner dimension of the

Torah—Kabbalah and Hassidism—is more likely to be awake to this phenomenon within his or her psyche.

² An example of this is the Lubavitcher *Rebbe*'s call to teach the gentile world to follow the seven Noahide laws the Torah obligates them to live by. Though the Torah obligates the Jewish people to teach the gentile world its God-given commandments, in previous generations, it was not possible to do this because of the dangers involved. Today, the world is ready and we witness many righteous gentiles who are most receptive and willing to define themselves as *B'nei Noach* ("children of Noah") according to the law of Moses. Nonetheless, antisemitism is still rampant, and indeed, many religions and creeds promulgate it and incite their followers against Jews and Judaism. To face, head on, antisemitism and combat it demands the greatest call to power. The *Rebbe* instructed us to do this by teaching all gentiles the seven Noahide laws. He did not approve of publicly debating religious issues; he believed fully in the adage, "a little light dispels much darkness [and much light transforms the darkness itself into light]."

³ Proverbs 28:14. The positive fear referred to here includes both the fear of God in general and the fear of sin (which severs us from God) in particular. As will be explained, maturity transforms fear physical or spiritual harm into natural carefulness, refining the intense emotion of fear and reserving it for the fear and awe of God.

The fear of God is one of the 248 *positive* commandments of the Torah: "You shall fear *God*, your God…" (Deuteronomy 6:13, 10:20). All positive commandments are motivated by the love of God. And so we are taught in Hassidism, that in truth, one's fear of God is an expression of one's love for Him. Ironically, one *loves* to *fear* God, and so, "*Happy* is the man who *fears* continuously."

In the future, the very essence of fear and trembling will become transformed into joy and laughter. This is alluded to in the phrase, "[God,] the fear of Isaac" (Genesis 31:42). Since the name *Isaac* in Hebrew means "shall laugh," this phrase reads literally, "Fear shall laugh." This is the ultimate example of sweetening.

⁴ It is indeed said of the Ba'al Shem Tov that he was never a child.

⁵ *Likutei Diburim* 385b; *Kuntres Chai Elul 5703*, p. 31.

6 Proverbs 22:13.

7 This is because the fear of God derives directly from the belief that "there is none beside Him" (Deuteronomy 4:35).

8 *Midrash Tehilim* 119:36.

9 See *Sha'ar HaYichud VehaEmunah*, ch. 1.

10 *Bereishit Rabbah* 10:6.

11 Rabbi Yosef Yitzchak Schneersohn (1880-1950) was the sixth *Rebbe* of Chabad-Lubavitch.

12 *Sefer HaToldot Admur HaRayatz*, vol. 3, introduction.

13 With the coming of *Mashiach*, the prophet tells that "a suckling will play on the hole of a serpent, and a weaned child will place his hand on the lair of a rattlesnake" (Isaiah 11:8). The snake, the arch-symbol of human fear, will become a source of "play" and delight. This is the third and final stage of sweetening, where the evil itself is transformed into good. Now, even before the coming of *Mashiach*, one can foretaste the delight of "playing with the snake" by studying the inner dimension of the Torah which reveals both the essential Divinity within all and the truth that, even now, "evil is the throne of good" (*Keter Shem Tov* 26, 188).

14 This is the mystical meaning of the phrase in Genesis 31:42, "the fear of Isaac," which may be read: "fear will laugh."

15 Psalms 34:15, 37:27.

16 Ecclesiastes 7:20.

17 See *Keter Shem Tov* 393.

18 *Likutei Sichot*, vol. 1, p. 124, vol. 2, p. 474.

19 *Chovot HaLevavot* 5:5; *Tanya*, ch. 12 (17a), based on Ecclesiastes 2:13.

20 In Hebrew, the root "to do" (*asah*) can also mean "to make."

21 *Keter Shem Tov* 41, 69, 89.

22 Since this is a departure from our habitual patterns of behavior, it requires extra effort. The effort required to break the mold is the "super-good" alluded to by the word "might" in the verse, "You shall love *God* your God with all your heart, with all your soul, and with all your *might*" (Deuteronomy 6:5). The Hebrew word for "your might" (*meodecha*) literally means "your very-much." Doing good this way is a messianic mode of action in that it liberates and redeems us from our accustomed level of existence.

23 *Yoma* 86b.

24 Rabbi Avraham Bornstein of Sochatchov (1839-1910) explains that it is a mistake to think that it is illegitimate to enjoy the performance of *mitzvah*, especially that of learning the Torah and revealing new insights into its meaning. The ultimate study of the Torah "for its own sake" is to study knowing that such is the will of God, together with experiencing great pleasure and satisfaction in one's learning and opportunity to innovate. Even when we study the Torah just for the sake of experiencing pleasure, we have performed the *mitzvah* of learning Torah in part (Introduction to *Eglei Tal*).

25 Even experiential channels permissible by Jewish law when sought *in place* of God enter the category of the forbidden (see *Tanya*, chapter 7, 27, quoting Nachmanides on Leviticus 19:2).

26 If J. is scholarly, perhaps when he comes across an interesting idea in his Torah studies that he would like to research or pursue, he pushes away the thought, saying, "I have no time for this; I have to first finish my daily study obligations I have set for myself, and then I have to work to provide for my family." Or perhaps he does not allow himself to become as engrossed in his prayers as he might like, for fear of missing work (during the week) or keeping his family waiting for him (on Shabbat).

27 As it is written, "for with You is the source of life" (Psalms 36:10). It is taught in Hassidism that the Hebrew word for "life" (*chaim*) here means "pleasure."

28 *ibid.*

29 *Avot* 1:6.

30 p. 43.

31 It is for this reason that in Jewish philosophy man is called "the speaker" (*medaber*) rather than "the thinker" or "the knower" (*maskil*). Significantly, the numerical value of the word *medaber* (246) is the same as that of the phrase used in the Bible to describe the uniqueness of humanity: we were created in "the image of God" (*tzelem Elokim*, Genesis 1:27, 9:6). Having been created in "the image of God," man is capable of emulating God; just as God created the world through speech, so is man able to rectify God's creation, to bring it to its Divinely intended consummation—to "sweeten" all of reality—though his own rectified speech.

³² *Nidah* 45b.

³³ The word for "man" (*adam*) is cognate to that for "silence" (*demamah*). The name of the first, archetypal man, Adam, was simply the word for "man" itself; the name of the first, archetypal woman, Eve (*Chavah*) is cognate to the word for "expression" (*chavah*, as in Psalms 19:3). God created man by breathing "into his nostrils the breath of life, and man became a living being" (Genesis 2:7). The literal translation of the words for "living being" is "a being of life [*chayah*]," and the word *chayah* is the root of the name "Eve" (*Chavah*). Thus, the process of becoming "a living being" alludes to the creation of man's feminine aspect. The *Targum* for "living being" is "a speaking spirit." (*Sefer HaMa'amarim 5659*, p. 3 ff. See *Sha'arei Ahavah v'Ratzon*, p. 203.)

Based on this, we may infer that silence and speech are the male and female sides of the dynamic of *chashmal* explained above (p. 11). In the context of the Ba'al Shem Tov's threefold process of spiritual growth, this means that submission is the male side while sweetening is the female side. In Kabbalah, the origin of submission in the soul is the state of selflessness characteristic of the *partzuf* of *Abba* ("father"), while the origin of sweetening is the joy characteristic of the *partzuf* of *Ima* ("mother"). Separation is the ability of the male to manifest his female component and the female to manifest her male component so that they may unite.

³⁴ This phenomenon is alluded to in Ecclesiastes 10:5: "...like an error proceeding from a ruler." The words "proceeding from a ruler" may be read: "emitted from a person [otherwise] in control."

³⁵ See the discussion of the two dimensions of the mouth in *The Mystery of Marriage*, pp. 171-175.

³⁶ Ecclesiastes 3:21.

³⁷ Psalms 116:15.

³⁸ Proverbs 25:16.

³⁹ *Chagigah* 14b.

⁴⁰ *Likutei Torah* (Arizal) on Genesis 3:1.

⁴¹ It is told that Elisha ben Avuyah saw a person ask his son to climb a tree and bring him some nestlings. The son, who obliged, fulfilled two commandments of the Torah at once: honoring his parent (Exodus 20:12, Deuteronomy 5:16) and sending away a mother bird from its nest before

taking its young (Deuteronomy 22:7). The reward explicitly promised for both of these commandments is long life, but the son accidentally fell from the tree and was killed. The anomaly was too much for Elisha ben Avuyah to bear. (The truth is that "long life" in the Torah includes the ongoing existence of the soul in the afterlife. See *Kidushin* 39b.)

[42] In the terminology of Kabbalah, Ben Azzai attempted to rectify the primordial sin with the power of *chochmah*, Ben Zoma with the power of *binah*, Elisha ben Avuyah with the power of the five states of *gevurah* inherent in *da'at*, and Rabbi Akiva with the power of the five states of *chesed* inherent in *da'at*.

[43] In the Mishnah (*Berachot* 9:5), the sages interpret the second verse of the *Shema*—"You shall love God…with all your *soul*…" (Deuteronomy 6:5) to mean that we should be willing to give up our life for God. Throughout his life, Rabbi Akiva aspired to do this. In Kabbalah, we are taught that the fire in the heart of Rabbi Akiva, his desire to sanctify God's Name and willing acceptance of being tortured to death out of his great love for God, ignites love and devotion in our hearts—feeling close to God—even in the darkess days of exile, and will continue to do so until the coming of the Messiah.

[44] Ezekiel 47:12.

[45] The root of *terufah*, r-f-h, means "to loosen" or "to relax."

[46] Cf. *Keter Shem Tov* 34, the Ba'al Shem Tov's explanation of the saying of Reish Lakish in *Menachot* 99ab: "Sometimes cessation from Torah study is its foundation."

[47] Furthermore, in Hebrew, the word for "leaf" (*aleh*) is derived from the root meaning "to rise" (*alah*) or "above" (*elyon*), alluding to the unconscious, or more precisely super-conscious, the aspect of the soul that transcends the rationality of the conscious mind.

[48] Psalms 1:1-3.

[49] *Sukah* 21b (on Psalms 1:3).

Chapter 8

[1] *Bereishit Rabbah* 1:1.

[2] p. 34.

³ The desire to sweeten reality immediately, without separating (or subduing) first, recalls the sin of those Israelites who attempted to proceed toward the Promised Land even after God had told them they were sentenced to wander for forty years in the desert (see Numbers 14:40-45.) Moses warned them that God would not be with them, and indeed, they were forthwith defeated in battle by the enemy nation opposing their way. This impetuosity is the root of most sins described in the Torah, even, at times, those of great and holy individuals. The psychological drive to push incautiously toward the end, an existential "lack of patience," originates in the same inability to deal with evil that motivates people to push (repress) their inner evil back into their subconscious. When people feel threatened by the evil within them, they feel pressured either to repress it (and thus avoid the separation process) or pretend it does not exist (and therefore indulge in it as if it were already "sweetened").

⁴ This is not to imply that the Torah's vision of reality is so ordered that it allows no room for occasional impetuosity or spontaneity, but that these exist paradoxically in the context of order, playing their indispensable role in the rectification of reality. This is the Kabbalistic concept of bringing the "lights of chaos" (*tohu*) into the "vessels of rectification" (*tikun*). This is allied to the union of "circular" lights (*igulim*) with the "direct" revelation (*yosher*).

⁵ Genesis 1:5.

⁶ This is especially evident with regard to the sexual practices the Torah forbids but secular culture perceives as a matter of preference.

⁷ The sages state that for every forbidden sensual pleasure God created, He created a similar permitted one (*Vayikra Rabbah* 22:10). It is therefore unnecessary to permit that which the Torah forbids in order to live life to its fullest.

⁸ "It is time to act for God; abrogate the Torah!" (Psalms 119:126).

⁹ See *Teshuvat HaShanah*, p. 253 ff.

¹⁰ *Sotah* 47a.

¹¹ *Yevamot* 20a.

¹² See *Tanya*, chapter 7.

¹³ Proverbs 3:6.

¹⁴ *Y. Kidushin* 4:12.

15 *Eitz Chaim, Sha'ar HaKelalim* 1.

Chapter 9

1 p. 3.

2 See also *Tanya*, Introduction, based on Proverbs 29:13, as interpreted by the sages of the Talmud (*Temurah* 16a).

3 Saying of Rabbi Dovber of Lubavitch (quoted in *Igrot Kodesh* of the *Rebbe*, vol. 4, #986).

4 "Man is born a wild donkey" (Job 11:12).

5 *Kelalei HaChinuch VehaHadrachah* 7.

6 See *The Mystery of Marriage*, ch. 2.

7 Ecclesiastes 9:11.

8 *Shabbat* 151b.

9 *Avot* 4:1.

10 *Me'or Einaim*, beginning of *Chukat; Toldot Yaakov Yosef*, end of *Terumah; Keter Shem Tov* 302; *Sefer HaSichot 5700* (summer), p. 83; see *Likutei Sichot*, vol. 10, pp. 24 ff. Thus, the Ba'al Shem Tov interpreted the apparent redundancy of the phrase, "Rebuke, you shall rebuke your fellow" (Leviticus 19:17) to mean: first rebuke (and correct) yourself, and then you will know how to rebuke (and correct) your fellow (*Keter Shem Tov* 131).

11 *HaYom Yom*, 3 *Iyar.*

12 *Sefer HaMa'amarim Kuntresim*, vol. 2, pp. 356b-358a (reprinted in *Igrot Kodesh Admor HaRayatz*, vol. 3, pp. 379 ff) and the discourse following (pp. 358b-363a). The author, Rabbi Yosef Yitzchak of Lubavitch, encouraged all his followers to study and integrate the lessons of this discourse (*HaYom Yom*, 24 *Tishrei*). The Talmudic terms for subjective identification and objective distance are "closeness of knowledge" (*kiruv hada'at*) and "cleanliness of knowledge" (*neki'ut hada'at*), respectively. See *Sha'arei Ahavah VeRatzon*, p. 203 ff.

13 Rabbi Dovber (1773-1827), the son of Rabbi Shneur Zalman of Liadi, was the second *Rebbe* of Chabad-Lubavitch.

14 In the terminology of Kabbalah, the patient's three stages of submission, separation, and sweetening correspond to the three final letters of God's Name *Havayah*: The final *hei* corresponds to the *sefirah* of

malchut, whose inner experience is that of lowliness and submission; the *vav* corresponds to the emotive attributes of the heart, where we must separate between good and evil; and the first *hei* corresponds to the *sefirah* of *binah*, the inner understanding of the heart, where all severities—psychological anxieties—are sweetened in their source. The silence of the counselor corresponds to the *yud*, the first letter of the Name *Havayah*, which corresponds to the *sefirah* of *chochmah*, of which it is said, "silence is a fence for wisdom" (*Avot* 3:13). The metaphysical union of the counselor and the counseled in therapy is the union of the two initial letters of the Name *Havayah*—the silence of the counselor and the sweetening speech of the patient—which is referred to in the *Zohar* (3:4a) as that of "two companions that never part."

15 The threefold inter-inclusion within sweetening is one of the clearest examples of the Ba'al Shem Tov's process of submission, separation, and sweetening that appears in his own teachings. He sees this inter-inclusion in the following passage from the Book of Psalms: "Guard your tongue from evil and your lips from speaking guile. Turn from evil and do good, seek peace and pursue it" (Psalms 34:14-15), which he reads as follows: "When you perceive evil in another, do not immediately rebuke him: *guard your tongue from [rebuking him for his] evil*. Rather, recognize that he is merely a mirror of yourself. This silence is an act of submission. Instead, *turn from [the] evil* in yourself—this is an act of separation. Then, *do good*, i.e., transform the evil into good—this is an act of sweetening within yourself. Finally, you can *seek peace and pursue it*, i.e., sweeten the other, helping him transform his evil into good" (*Toldot Yaakov Yosef* in the name of the Ba'al Shem Tov, quoted in *Asifat Amarim* on Psalms 34:14-15.)

3. sweetening	speech	helping the other person tranform his evil into good
		Transforming the evil within yourself into good
2. separation	severing	turning from the evil within yourself
1. submission	silence	holding your tongue from rebuke
		seeing the other as a mirror of yourself

16 p. 1.

17 *Avot* 1:6, 16.

18 See *Tzetl Katan* 13.

19 *Uktzin* 3:12; Psalms 29:11.

Chapter 10

1 *Chagigah* 13a.

2 Liturgy, last blessing of the *Amidah*.

3 In the words of the sages: "[If one says] 'I have toiled and not found,' do not believe him…[If one says] 'I have toiled and I have found,' believe him" (*Megilah* 6b).

4 See *Tanya*, introduction (4a).

5 By analogy, the "deeper" forms of art and music are those that express conflict and yearning, in contrast to those that express joy or celebration. In the statement of the *Zohar* quoted further on—"weeping is wedged in my heart on this side, and joy is wedged in my heart on the other"—the numerical value of the word for "weeping" (*bechiyah*, 37) is the same as that of the name of the highest level of the soul, *yechidah*, while the numerical value of the word for "joy" (*chedvah*, 23) is the same as that of the name of the second highest level of the soul, *chayah*.

6 Isaiah 2:3.

7 Maimonides' commentary to *Sanhedrin* 10:1.

8 The sages express the intensity of concern we are to have over hastening the coming of the Messiah with the words: "any generation in which the Temple is not rebuilt in its days is considered as though it itself destroyed it!" (*Y. Yoma* 1:1).

9 *Sefer HaSichot 5751*, vol. 2, p. 474.

10 This includes the fact that they *cannot* be perfect, as it is written, "there is no righteous man on earth that does good and does not sin" (Ecclesiastes 7:20), as mentioned above (p. 76). Recognizing this truth in himself, the *tzadik* develops true empathy with others, regardless of their spiritual state.

11 The more righteous the individual, the more acutely will he feel this anxiety. This is because the closer a person comes in his consciousness to

God, the more profoundly is he aware of his existential nothingness and inability to conceive of God's essence (*Igeret HaKodesh* 2).

¹² *Derech Chaim* 35a ff.

¹³ *Zohar* 3:75a; *Tanya*, end of ch. 34.

¹⁴ Thus, the numerical value of the Hebrew for "anxiety in the heart of man" equals that of *Mashiach* (358).

¹⁵ *Me'or Einayim, Pinchas*, in the name of the Ba'al Shem Tov; *Likutei Sichot*, vol. 2, p. 599, 692, etc.

¹⁶ *Sanhedrin* 97a.

¹⁷ Habakkuk 2:3.

¹⁸ Malachi 3:1.

Chapter 11

¹ This letter was originally published in Rabbi Yaakov Yosef of Polnoye's *Ben Porat Yosef*. The relevant portion of it is reproduced at the beginning of *Keter Shem Tov*.

² This motif is preeminent in the writings of Rabbi Shneur Zalman of Liadi. Many of his discourses begin with theme of remembering the descent of one's soul from its primordial state of standing in God's presence above to enter a physical body—detached by its very nature from Divine consciousness—below.

³ The prophets referred to this state of absolute presence when they swore by "God, before whom I stood" (1 Kings 17:1, 18:15, 2 Kings 3:14, 5:16).

⁴ See *HaYom Yom*, 3 *Elul*.

⁵ *Nidah* 30b.

⁶ *Kitzurim v'He'arot L'Tanya*, pp. 66 ff.

⁷ Only in the messianic future will the prophecy, "and *all* Your people are *tzadikim*" (Isaiah 60:21) be fulfilled literally.

⁸ Indeed, in the Talmud (*Rosh HaShanah* 16b), we find that on Rosh Hashanah, God opens three books: the Book of the Righteous, the Book of the Wicked, and the Book of the Intermediates.

⁹ The second section of the *Tanya, Sha'ar HaYichud VehaEmunah* ["The Gate to Unity and Faith"] was originally printed together with the

first part of the *Tanya*, "The Book of the Intermediates," for it was seen by the author to complement it. *Sha'ar HaYichud VehaEmunah* describes in depth the theological underpinnings of the first part of the *Tanya*.

In addition, in Rabbi Shneur Zalman's subsequent works, *Torah Or* and *Likutei Torah*, he seems in many cases to be addressing the reader as if he had already passed beyond the struggle of the *beinoni* and is involved in the spiritual world of the *tzadik*.

[10] Rabbi Elimelech of Lizhensk (1717-1787) was a disciple of the Maggid of Mezritch and one of the founders of Hassidism in Galicia. *Noam Elimelech* is considered the seminal work of what is known as the "general" stream of Hassidism.

[11] Spontaneous conversation with God (known in the Breslov tradition as *hitbodedut*, "self-isolation [with God]") is a natural component of all other Hassidic paths, as well. It is said of the followers of Rabbi Shneur Zalman of Liadi, the founder of the Chabad school, that they would spend more time in the fields, alone with God in meditation and conversation, than in town.

[12] *Cf.* the beginning of Rabbi Dovber of Lubavitch's *Derech Chaim*, where it is stated that God derives pleasure from the endeavors of the wicked to better their ways.

[13] See *Tzetl Katan* 13.

[14] In his letter to his brother-in-law mentioned above (p. 123), the Ba'al Shem Tov relates how the *Mashiach* told him that he will come only when the Ba'al Shem Tov succeeds in inspiring others to reach his level and they can "sweeten" the bitter through holy intentions on Divine Names. Thus, the ultimate vision of the Ba'al Shem Tov is that as many people as possible reach the level of *tzadik* and become able to sweeten the bitter.

[15] The *Chabad* approach requires that people work on themselves with their own faculties, yet be aware that their power and inspiration derive from the *Rebbe*. In this way, they augment their spiritual connection and devotion to the *Rebbe* all the more.

[16] We see that—in contrast to the other two streams of Hassidism— in the school of Rabbi Elimelech, many disciples came to the *Rebbe* with the tacit understanding that they would one day assume the mantle of leadership themselves. Indeed, the court of Rabbi Elimelech (and that of

his disciple Rabbi Yaakov Yitzchak, the "seer" of Lublin) branched out to become hundreds of Hassidic dynasties, the majority of which in turn continued to branch out, leading to the proliferation of Hassidic dynasties that have developed over time.

[17] As it is written, "He has redeemed my soul in peace from battle…" (Psalms 55:19). Rabbi Shneur Zalman was reading this verse when he was informed of his release from czarist prison on the 19th of Kislev 5559 (1799). Since then, this verse has become the leitmotif of the annual celebration of his release and has been expounded upon at length by the successive generations of Chabad *rebbe*s. In this way, the life-task of the *tzadik* has been made accessible to all of us.

[18] This is also why this branch of Hassidism places great emphasis on rectifying the "sins of youth," i.e., sexual sins. Rabbi Nachman's specific remedy for this all-inclusive sin (his *Tikun HaKelali*, literally, "the general rectification") consists of saying ten designated psalms corresponding to the ten expressions of song used the Book of Psalms. As we noted above (p. 39), the stage of spiritual growth expressed by reciting psalms is sweetening within submission.

[19] Rabbi Nachman's story of *The Fly and the Spider* (story #7 in *Sipurei Ma'asiyot*).

[20] The nurturing of this parent-child relationship with God is prescribed in chapter 44 of *Tanya* (63b).

[21] See *Tanya*, introduction (4a). The "of sorts" is explained more fully in the last section of this chapter.

[22] *Keter Shem Tov* 26, 188.

[23] *Berachot* 21a. "The early pietists would meditate an hour before prayer, pray for an hour, and meditate for an hour after prayer" three times a day (*Berachot* 32b).

[24] And indeed, in the closing passage of "The Book of Intermediates," Rabbi Shneur Zalman refers to the transformation of behavior in the *beinoni* by the same term he previously reserved for the transformation of the psyche in the *tzadik*, *ithapcha*.

[25] in chapters 1, 9, and 10.

[26] Psalms 109:22.

[27] *Y. Berachot* 9:5.

Chapter 12

[1] 2 Samuel 23:1.

[2] *Ibid.* 6:22.

[3] *Avodah Zarah* 4b-5a.

[4] Acronym of Rabbi *Sh*lomo ben *Yi*tzchak (1040-1105).

[5] Proverbs 5:18-20.

[6] Job 32:7-8.

[7] As Rabbi Meir—who was the Messiah-figure of the tannaitic period—said: "Look not at the flask but at what is in it. There is a new flask filled with old [wine], and an old [flask] empty even of new [wine]" (*Avot* 4:20).

[8] Elihu's name is sometimes written such that it can be read as Eliahu (the Hebrew for Elijah). The numerical vlaue of his full name, *Elihu ben Berachel* (358), is the same as the numerical value of the Hebrew for "Messiah," *Mashiach.*

[9] Rabbi Moses ben Nachman (1194-1270).

[10] Rabbi Shneur Zalman of Liadi told his son, Rabbi Dovber of Lubavitch, that in order to properly counsel someone, he must see the origin of his own soul in *Adam Kadmon* ("Primordial Man"), the Kabbalistic analog to the comprehensive soul of Adam. When Rabbi Dovber heard this, dumbfounded by the awesomeness of this requirement, he fainted and remained ill for many weeks.

[11] Ecclesiastes 12:13.

[12] *Avot* 4:15.

Index

A

Adam, 143
Adolescence, 25
  spiritual, 129
Akiva, Rabbi
  orchard, 85
  positive thinking, 53
Amidah. See prayer.
Anxiety. *See also* submission, separation, sweetening.
  and ego, 27
  and inner dimension of Torah, 111
  and the Messiah, 115
  blame for, 35
  cause of negative self-definition, 20
  King Solomon's advice, 16
  local vs. non-local solution, 59, 65
  obsession over, 27
  origin of, 15
  positive, 111
  suppression, ignoring, articulation, 16
Articulating anxiety
  as a form of relief, 56
  sweetening, 21

K

Kabbalah
  and anxiety, 15
  and depression, 29
  and evil, 23, 60
  cosmology of, 22
  evil, 85
  revelation of, xiii
  self-knowledge in, 4

L

Leaf, 87, 89
  Divine providence, 62
Life, purpose of, 5
Light
  dispels darkness, 81
Light and darkness
  submission, separation, sweetening, 10
Likutei Moharan, 127

M

Maccabees, 75
Marriage, 103
Maturity, 71, 129
  Kabbalistic paradigm, 22
Meditation
  general vs. detailed, 31
  meditative prayer, 48
Mentor. *See* therapist.
Messiah, 114
  as psychologist, 141

CPSIA information can be obtained
at www.ICGtesting.com
Printed in the USA
LVHW092147010321
680333LV00003B/13